HMH Georgia Science

This Write-In Book belongs to

_____

Teacher/Room

_____

Houghton Mifflin Harcourt™

Consulting Authors

Michael A. DiSpezio
Global Educator
North Falmouth, Massachusetts

Marjorie Frank
*Science Writer and Content-Area Reading
    Specialist*
Brooklyn, New York

Michael Heithaus
Dean, College of Arts and Sciences
Florida International University
North Miami, Florida

Georgia Reviewers

C. Alex Alvarez, Ed.D
Director of STEM and Curriculum
Valdosta City Schools
Valdosta, Georgia

Kristen N. Brooks
2nd Grade Teacher
Lindsey Elementary School
Warner Robins, Georgia

Melissa Davis
K–5 Science Coordinator
Atlanta Public Schools
Atlanta, Georgia

Natasha Luster-Knighton
5th Grade Science Teacher
Radium Springs Elementary
Albany, Georgia

Amy Materne
Russell Elementary School
Warner Robins, Georgia

Erin Neal
2nd Grade Teacher
White Oak Elementary School
Newnan, Georgia

Mark Christian Rheault
K–5 Specialist
Union County Elementary
Blairsville, Georgia

Kolenda Thomas-McDavis
5th Grade Science Ambassador
Northside Elementary
Warner Robins, Georgia

Christina Voigt
Teacher
Lake Joy Elementary
Warner Robins, Georgia

Dora A. Waite
Georgia State Science Ambassador
Russell Elementary
Warner Robins, Georgia

Contents

Track Your Progress

Levels of Inquiry Key ■ DIRECTED ■ GUIDED ■ INDEPENDENT

THE NATURE OF SCIENCE AND S.T.E.M.

EARTH AND SPACE SCIENCE

LIFE SCIENCE

PHYSICAL SCIENCE

Work Like a Scientist

© Houghton Mifflin Harcourt Publishing Company (bg) © James Schwabel / Alamy Stock Photo; (inset) ©James Quine / Alamy / Corbis / CNB/ce/Age Fotestock

Big Idea

Scientists ask questions about the world around them. They find answers by investigating through many methods.

Thomas Edison's lab

I Wonder Why

Scientists use tools to find out about things. Why?

Turn the page to find out.

Here's Why Tools help scientists learn more than they could with just their senses.

In this unit, you will explore this Big Idea, the Essential Questions, and the Investigations on the Inquiry Flipchart.

Levels of Inquiry Key ■ DIRECTED ■ GUIDED ■ INDEPENDENT

Track Your Progress

Big Idea Scientists ask questions about the world around them. They find answers by investigating through many methods.

Essential Questions

Now I Get the Big Idea!

Science Notebook

Before you begin each lesson, be sure to write your thoughts about the Essential Question.

Essential Question

How Do We Use Inquiry Skills?

Engage Your Brain!

Find the answer in this lesson.

You tell how these flowers are alike and different.

You are

_____ them.

Active Reading

Lesson Vocabulary

1 Preview the lesson.

2 Write the vocabulary term here.

_____

Use Inquiry Skills

Inquiry skills help people find out information. Inquiry skills help people plan and do tests.

These children use inquiry skills to do a task for school. They are observing. Observe means to use your five senses to learn about things.

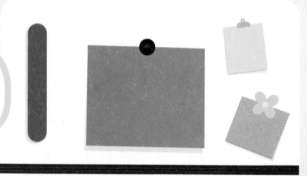

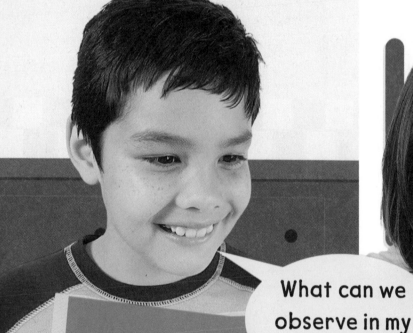

What can we observe in my backyard?

Danny and Sophie want to observe things in the backyard. They plan an investigation. They plan how to find out what they want to know. They also predict, or make a good guess, about what they will observe.

▶ This page names three inquiry skills. Circle the name for one of the skills.

Explore the Backyard

Danny and Sophie head out to the backyard to begin their task. Danny finds the length and the height of the birdhouse. He measures it with a ruler.

Active Reading

Find the sentence that explains what it means to **measure**. Draw a line under the sentence.

They use inquiry skills to learn more about the backyard.

Sophie compares leaves. She observes how they are alike and how they are different. She may also classify, or sort, many leaves in the backyard by the way they are alike.

▶ Look at Sophie's leaves. Put them in order of size from smallest to largest.

_____ _____ _____

Model and Infer

Now Danny and Sophie draw a map of the backyard. They are making a model to show what something is like. You could also make a model to show how something works.

My Backyard

birch tree

rose bush

maple tree

bird bath

bird house

© Houghton Mifflin Harcourt Publishing Company

Active Reading

Find the sentences that explain what it means to **make a model**.
Draw a line under the sentences.

Danny and Sophie use one more inquiry skill.
They infer. They use what they know to answer
a question—Are there any living things in
the backyard? They can infer that the backyard
is home to many plants and animals.

▶ Think about what you know about winter.
Infer what Danny and Sophie might
observe in the backyard during winter.

_____

_____

Sum It Up!

1 Complete It!

Fill in the blank.

How are measuring, observing, and predicting alike?

They are all

_____ .

2 Circle It!

Circle the skill name to match the meaning.

Which one means to choose steps you will do to learn something?

infer

plan an investigation

classify

3 Draw and Write It!

Observe something outside. Then draw and write to record your observations.

_____

_____

 # Brain Check

Name _____

Word Play

Read each clue below. Then unscramble the letters to write the correct answer.

observe	compare	measure	infer

1 to find the size or amount of something

s e m a r e u _____

2 to use your senses to learn about something

b o s r e e v _____

3 to observe how things are alike and different

p o c r a m e _____

4 to use what you know to answer a question

f n i r e _____

Match each inquiry skill to its meaning.

to make a good guess about what will happen	plan an investigation
to sort things by how they are alike	classify
to show what something is like or how it works	predict
to follow steps to answer a question	make a model

Family Members: See *ScienceSaurus*® for more information about observations and investigations.

Essential Question

How Do We Use Science Tools?

Engage Your Brain!

Find the answer to the question in the lesson.

What does a thermometer measure?

_____

Active Reading

Lesson Vocabulary

1 Preview the lesson.

2 Write the two vocabulary terms here.

_____   _____

Top Tools

You use tools every day. Tools are things that help you do a job. **Science tools** help you find out information.

A hand lens is one science tool. It helps you observe more details than with your eyes alone.

> ▶ What can you see through this hand lens? Circle it.

A hand lens makes things look larger.

Measuring Tools

You use some tools for measuring things. You use a **thermometer** to measure temperature. You use a measuring cup to measure amounts of liquids.

A thermometer measures temperature in units called degrees.

A measuring cup measures liquids in units called milliliters, cups, and ounces.

Measure More!

You use a tool called a scale to measure weight. You can use a balance to measure mass.

This scale measures weight in units called pounds and ounces.

▶ Name two things you can weigh on a scale.

_____

_____

This balance measures mass in units called grams and kilograms.

You use a ruler and a tape measure to measure distance as well as length, width, and height. Both tools measure in units called inches or centimeters.

Circle the object the ruler is measuring.

A ruler measures objects with straight lines.

A tape measure can measure around an object.

Sum It Up!

① Answer It!

Write the answer to this question.

You want to measure how much water fits into a pail. What tool could you use?

_____

② Draw It!

Draw yourself using a measuring tool.

③ Mark It!

Mark an X on the tool that does <u>not</u> measure.

Brain Check

Name _____

Word Play

Match the name of each tool to its picture.

tape measure	
balance	
thermometer	
measuring cup	
hand lens	

Apply Concepts

Name the tool you could use for each job.

measuring the length of a book	_____
finding the weight of a watermelon	_____
observing curves and lines on the tip of your finger	_____

Take It Home!

Family Members: Go on a scavenger hunt. See which tools from this lesson you have in or around your home. Discuss with your child how to use each tool.

1

In 1742, Celsius invented the Celsius scale to measure temperature.

2

The temperature at which water freezes on the Celsius scale is 0°.

4

Things to Know About

Anders Celsius

3

The temperature at which water boils on the Celsius scale is 100°.

4

Celsius was an astronomer, or a person who studies the stars and other things in space.

Celsius Match Up

1

► Read each thermometer. Write the number that matches the correct temperature in each picture.

2

3

► How does a temperature scale help you tell about the weather?

_____

_____

Name _____

Essential Question

What Tools Can We Use?

Set a Purpose

Write what you want to find out.

_____

_____

Think About the Procedure

1 Which science tool did you choose? What does it do?

_____

_____

2 How will the tool help you observe the object?

_____

_____

Record Your Data

Record your observations in this chart.

| My Object _____ |
| My Tool _____ |

What I Learned Without the Tool	What I Learned With the Tool

Draw Conclusions

How can a science tool help you learn more about an object?

_____

_____

_____

Ask More Questions

What other questions can you ask about how science tools are used?

_____

_____

_____

24

Essential Question

How Do Scientists Think?

Engage Your Brain!

Find the answer in the lesson.

When scientists _____ they follow steps and use tools to answer a question.

Active Reading

Lesson Vocabulary

1 Preview the lesson.

2 Write the four vocabulary terms here.

_____ _____

_____ _____

Let's Observe It!

Scientists **investigate**. They plan and do a test to answer a question or solve a problem. They use inquiry skills and science tools to help them.

There are many ways to investigate. But many scientists follow a sequence, or order of events. Here's one possible sequence. First, scientists may observe and ask a question.

Active Reading

Clue words can help you find the order of things. **First** is a clue word. Circle this clue word in the paragraph above.

Does food coloring spread faster in cold water or warm water?

cold

▶ What objects will these children use for their test? Circle them.

Now, scientists can make a hypothesis. A **hypothesis** is a statement that can be tested. Then scientists plan a fair test. The scientists list the materials they will need and the steps they will take to do their test.

Food coloring spreads faster in warm water.

food coloring

warm

Let's Test It!

Next, the scientists are ready to do their test. They follow their plan and record what they observe.

Active Reading

Clue words can help you find the order of things. **Next** is a clue word. Circle this clue word in the paragraph above.

These children test whether food coloring spreads faster in cold water or warm water.

After the test, scientists **draw conclusions**.
They use the information they have gathered to
decide if their results support the hypothesis.
Finally, they write or draw to **communicate** what
they learned.

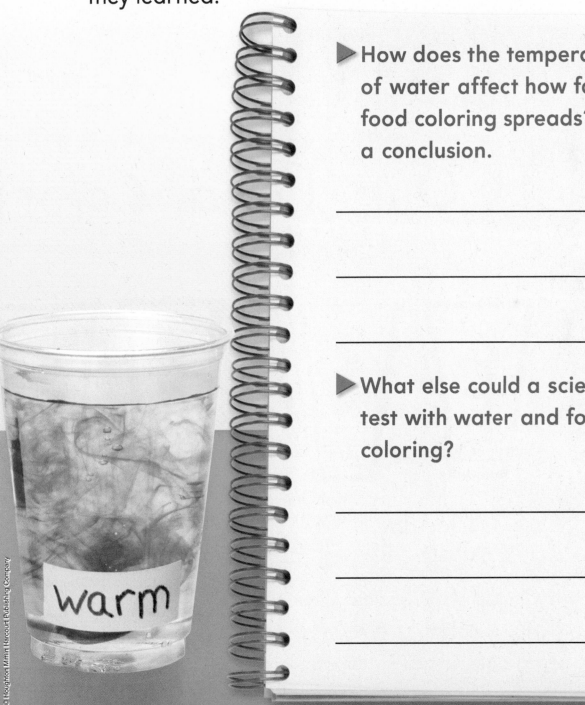

▶ How does the temperature
of water affect how fast the
food coloring spreads? Draw
a conclusion.

_____

_____

_____

▶ What else could a scientist
test with water and food
coloring?

_____

_____

_____

warm

Let's Check Again!

Scientists do the same test a few times. They need to make sure that they get similar results every time. In this investigation, the food coloring should spread faster in warm water every time.

Our Food Colori

cold   warm   cold   warm

Monday   Wednesday

► Look at the **warm** cup for both Monday and Friday. Draw a conclusion. Color in the **warm** cup for Wednesday to show what it should look like.

Test

cold

warm

Friday

Do the Math!

Measure Length

Choose an object. Use a ruler to measure the object's length. Measure it three times. Record.

Length of _____	
Measure 1	
Measure 2	
Measure 3	

1. How do your numbers compare?

_____

_____

2. Why do you think so?

_____

_____

_____

Sum It Up!

① Order It!

Number the steps from 1 to 4 to tell a way scientists investigate.

_____ Observe and ask a question.

_____ Do the test and record what happens.

_____ Draw conclusions and communicate.

_____ Make a hypothesis and plan a fair test.

② Circle It!

Circle the correct answer.

Suppose you make a poster to show the results of your test. You are _____.

observing   planning your test

making a hypothesis   communicating

Brain Check

Lesson **4**

Name _____

Word Play

Circle the word to complete each sentence.

1. You use inquiry skills and science tools to learn. You _____.

   communicate   investigate

2. You take the first step to do an investigation. You _____.

   draw conclusions   observe

3. You make a statement that you can test. You make a _____.

   hypothesis   conclusion

4. You use information you gathered to explain what you learned. You _____.

   draw conclusions   observe

5. You write to tell about the results of a test. You _____.

   communicate   ask a question

© Houghton Mifflin Harcourt Publishing Company

33

Apply Concepts

These steps show a test some children did.
Label each box with a step from this lesson.

The children look at an ice cube. They ask—
Will it melt in the sun?

Observe and _____.

They form a statement that the ice cube will melt
in the sun.

_____.

They follow their plan. The ice cube melts! They
decide that the sun's heat caused the ice to melt.

Test and _____.

The children write and draw to tell the results
of their test.

_____.

Family Members: Work with your child to plan an
investigation. Use the steps from this lesson.

Name _____

Essential Question

How Do We Solve a Problem?

Set a Purpose

What problem do you want to solve?

_____

_____

Think About the Procedure

1 Why do you make a list of the properties the holder must have?

_____

_____

2 Why do you design your holder before you build it?

_____

_____

Record Your Data

Record the details of your plan in this chart.

The Problem	
My Plan	
Materials I need	

Draw Conclusions

Sometimes it is helpful to make a model first before making the real thing. How can making a model help you solve a problem?

_____

_____

Ask More Questions

What other questions do you have about designing and making models to solve problems?

_____

_____

Unit 1 Review

Vocabulary Review

Use the terms in the box to complete the sentences.

| communicate |
| investigate |
| thermometer |

1. When you draw or write, you
   _____.

2. A tool that measures temperature is a(n)
   _____.

3. When you plan and do a test to answer a question, you _____.

Science Concepts

Fill in the letter of the choice that best answers the question.

4. Sumeet looks at the sky before he goes to school. It is dark and cloudy outside. What skill is Sumeet using?
   Ⓐ comparing
   Ⓑ inferring
   Ⓒ observing

5. Victor weighs a melon on a scale. The melon weighs 3 pounds. Ana also measures the weight of the same melon. What should Ana observe?
   Ⓐ The melon weighs 2 pounds.
   Ⓑ The melon weighs 3 pounds.
   Ⓒ The melon weighs 4 pounds.

6. Reem uses this tool to find the length of a book.

| 1 2 3 4 5 6 7 8 9 10 11 12 |
| centimeters |

What is she doing?

Ⓐ classifying

Ⓑ inferring

Ⓒ measuring

7. Jia wants to find out how the temperature in the afternoon compares to the morning temperature. What should she do?

Ⓐ Infer the afternoon temperature. Then compare it to the morning temperature.

Ⓑ Measure the afternoon temperature. Then compare it to the morning temperature.

Ⓒ Predict the afternoon temperature. Then compare it to the morning temperature.

8. Lea investigates the answer to a question. Then she repeats her experiment. Which will **most likely** be true?

Ⓐ The results will be the same.

Ⓑ The results will be different.

Ⓒ She cannot compare the results.

9. Carlos finishes an investigation. He draws this picture in a notebook.

Why does Carlos draw the picture?

Ⓐ to plan the investigation

Ⓑ to predict what will happen

Ⓒ to record what he observed

10. Jared knows that his two blocks are the same color but different shapes. How does he know?

(A) He measures them.

(B) He makes a model.

(C) He observes and compares them.

11. You think that an ant and a butterfly have the same parts. Why would models help you find out if this is true?

(A) The models would be the same size as the real insects.

(B) The models would show parts that the real insects have.

(C) Making models would mean that you do not have to make observations.

12. Kate wants to know whether a tree or a bush is taller. Which tool should she use?

(A)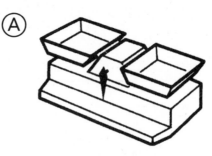

(B)

(C)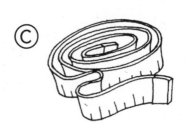

Inquiry and the Big Idea

Write the answers to these questions.

13. You complete an investigation about plants. Now you have another question. What should you do?

_____

_____

14. Look at the picture.

a. What science tool is the boy using?

_____

b. What is he doing?

_____

Technology and Our World

The Pyramids,
Indianapolis, Indiana

Big Idea

Engineers use a process to design new technology to meet human needs. Technology affects our everyday life and can affect the environment around us.

I Wonder How

An engineer planned a design for these buildings. How?
Turn the page to find out.

Here's How An engineer drew a plan for the buildings. The plan showed these interesting shapes.

In this unit, you will explore this Big Idea, the Essential Questions, and the Investigations on the Inquiry Flipchart.

Levels of Inquiry Key ■ DIRECTED ■ GUIDED ■ INDEPENDENT

Track Your Progress

Big Idea Engineers use a process to design new technology to meet human needs. Technology affects our everyday life and can affect the environment around us.

Essential Questions

Now I Get the Big Idea!

Science Notebook

Before you begin each lesson, be sure to write your thoughts about the Essential Question.

Essential Question

What Is the Design Process?

Engage Your Brain!

Find the answer to the question in the lesson.

How could you keep the dog leashes from getting tangled?

You could _____ _____.

Active Reading

Lesson Vocabulary

1. Preview the lesson.

2. Write the two vocabulary terms here.

_____ _____

Get Real!

Look at the engineers at work!
Engineers solve problems by using math and science. The answers they find help people.

Engineers work in many areas. Some engineers design cars. Some make robots. Others find ways to make the world cleaner or safer.

Active Reading

Find the sentence that tells the meaning of **engineers**. Draw a line under that sentence.

A civil engineer plans bridges and roads.

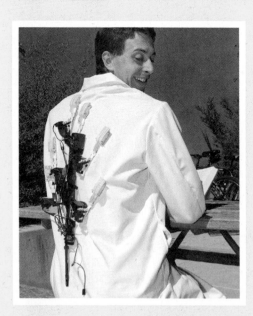

A robotics engineer designs robots.

The Design Process

How do engineers solve a problem? They use a design process. A **design process** is a set of steps that engineers follow to solve problems.

This engineer checks on a building project.

▶ Circle the names of three kinds of engineers.

An aerospace engineer may work on airplanes or rockets.

A Tangled Mess!

When Kate walks her dogs, their leashes always get tangled. She needs to solve this problem. How can a design process help?

1 Find a Problem

Kate's first step is to name her problem. What is wrong? What does she want to do? Then Kate brainstorms ways to solve her problem.

Active Reading

Things may happen in order. Write 1 next to what happens first. Write 2 next to what happens next.

Kate gets out her Science Notebook. She will keep good records. She will show how she plans and builds the solution to her problem.

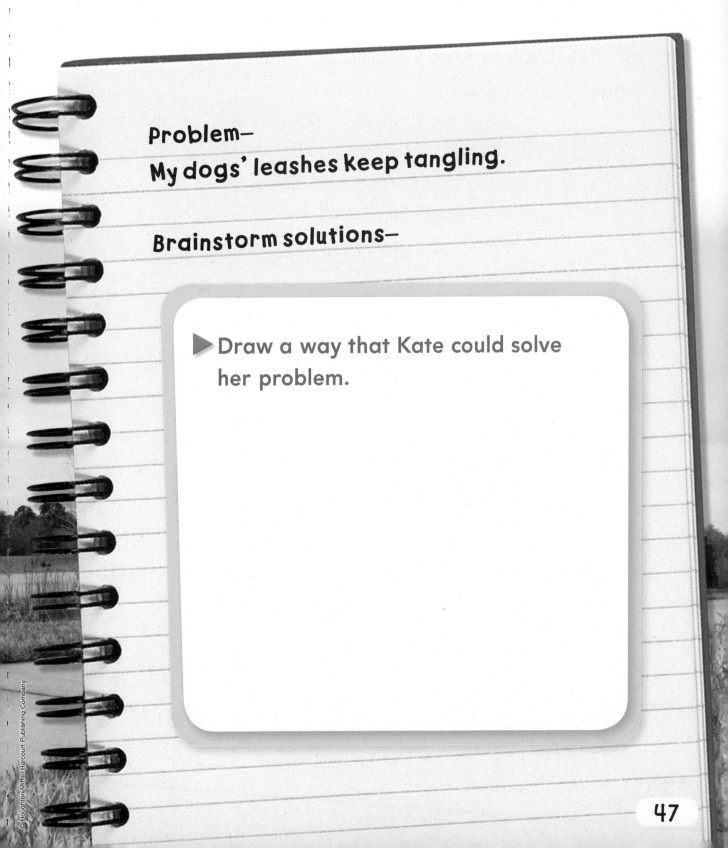

Problem—
My dogs' leashes keep tangling.

Brainstorm solutions—

▶ Draw a way that Kate could solve her problem.

2 Plan and Build

Next, Kate chooses a solution to try. She makes a plan. She draws and labels her plan.

Kate chooses materials that are good for leashes. Look at Kate's materials. What materials would you choose?

Active Reading

Clue words can help you find the order of things. **Next** is a clue word. Draw a box around this clue word.

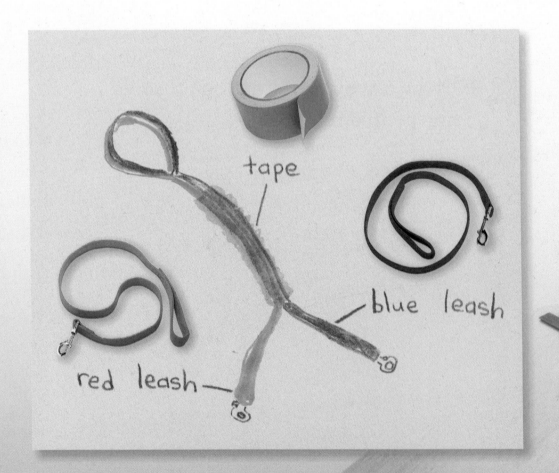

tape

blue leash

red leash

Kate follows her plan to make her new leash.
The new leash may be the solution to her problem!

▶ How does planning help Kate build her new leash?

_____

_____

③ Test and Improve

It is time for Kate to find out whether the new leash works. She tests it when she walks the dogs. Kate will know the leash works if it does not tangle.

4 Redesign

Kate thinks of ways to improve her new leash. She writes notes about how to make her design better.

5 Communicate

Kate shows the results of her test. She takes a picture of her design. She also writes about what happened during the test.

Ways to make the design better—make the leash parts or the handle longer.

My Results—
1. Red and blue parts of the new leash did not tangle.
2. My feet bumped the dogs as I walked.

▶ Circle the part of the results that tells about a problem with the leash.

Sum It Up!

① Circle It!

Circle the step of the design process shown here.

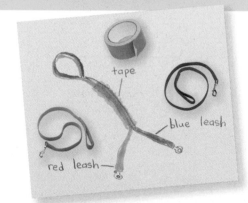

Test and Improve

Plan and Build

Find a Problem

② Write It!

Write the answer to the question.

Why is it important to keep good records?

_____

_____

_____

_____

Word Play

Write a term for each definition.

| design process | materials | solution | test |

steps that engineers follow to solve a problem

__ __ __ __ __ __   __ __ __ __ __ __ __
   1   3 2

the answer to a problem

__ __ __ __ __ __ __ __
         4   5

how you find out whether a solution works

__ __ __ __
  6

things you use to make a design

__ __ __ __ __ __ __ __ __
    7 8

Solve the riddle. Write the numbered letters in order on the lines below.

I am a scientist who uses math and science to solve problems. Who am I?

__ __ __ __ __ __ __ __
1 2 3 4 5 6 7 8

Complete the flowchart with the steps of the design process.

Design Process

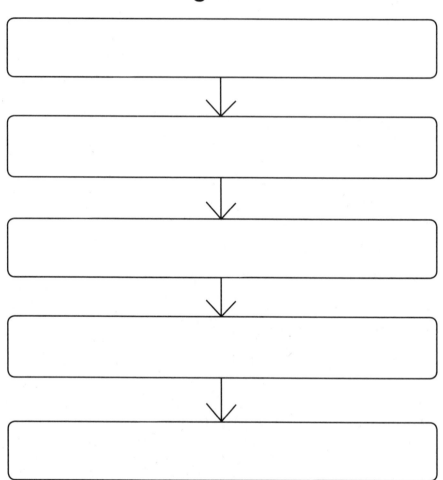

Family Members: See *ScienceSaurus*® for more information about engineers and technology.

Take It Home!

Inquiry Flipchart p. 8

Name _____

How Can We Use the Design Process?

Set a Purpose

Tell what you want to do.

_____

_____

Think About the Procedure

1 Why do you need to plan your solution?

_____

_____

_____

2 Why do you need to test your solution?

_____

_____

Record Your Data

Draw to communicate your solution and the test results. Label the materials. Write a caption to tell how your solution works.

Draw Conclusions

How did the design process help you solve the problem?

_____

_____

Ask More Questions

What other questions could you ask about using the design process?

_____

_____

Essential Question

What Is Technology?

🧠 Engage Your Brain!

Find the answer to the question in the lesson.

You use the technology in this picture every day. What is it?

It is a

_____ .

Active Reading

Lesson Vocabulary

1 Preview the lesson.

2 Write the two vocabulary terms here.

_____ _____

By Design

Did you use a toothbrush or turn on a light today? Both a toothbrush and a light are kinds of technology. **Technology** is what engineers make to meet needs and solve problems. Anything people design to help us do things is technology.

Active Reading

Find the sentence that tells the meaning of **technology**. Draw a line under the sentence.

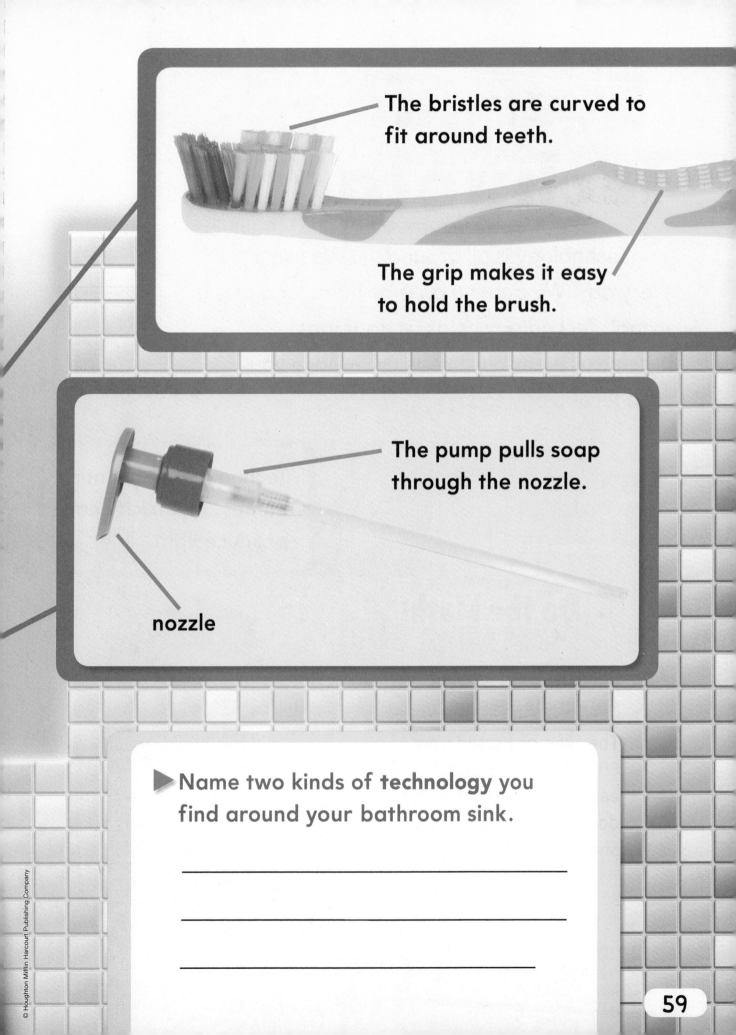

The bristles are curved to fit around teeth.

The grip makes it easy to hold the brush.

The pump pulls soap through the nozzle.

nozzle

▶ Name two kinds of **technology** you find around your bathroom sink.

_____

_____

_____

Everyday Technology

Technology is all around us. We use it every day. We depend on it at home and at school. Technology helps us do things. It helps us meet our needs. How have you used technology today?

Technology lights our homes. Electricity can produce light.

Do the Math!
Solve a Problem

Read the word problem. Answer the question.

The average person uses 80 gallons of water at home each day. How much water does a person use in 2 days? Show your work.

_____ gallons

▶ When the power goes out, so do electric lights. What other technology could you use to light your home?

_____

_____

Technology helps bring clean water to our homes.

Technology helps us make food. An oven, stovetop, and microwave oven cook food and heat water.

Play It Safe

Technology can be helpful when we use it with care. It can be unsafe if we do not use it with care.

We should use each kind of technology the way it was designed to be used. We should wear safety gear if we need to. Using technology correctly helps us stay safe.

Active Reading

The main idea is the most important idea about something. Draw two lines under the main idea.

The things that keep us safe are technology, too!

The hard plastic keeps things out of the eyes.

Foam and the hard covering protect the head.

Straps hold the helmet in place.

▶ What technology keeps you safe in a car?

_____

_____

_____

Environmental Effects

Technology can affect the environment. An **environment** is all the living and nonliving things in a place.

Batteries, for example, are a helpful technology. They provide power to phones, cars, toys, and other things. But they can harm the environment, too.

When old batteries break down, they can pollute water and soil.

Some batteries can be used over and over again. Most batteries can be recycled. How do you think this helps the environment?

▶ Write two ways you can keep batteries from being thrown away.

_____

_____

_____

Sum It Up!

① Circle It!

Circle the examples of technology.

② Write It!

Write a way people depend on technology.

_____

_____

_____

③ Draw It

Draw a way you use technology to be safe.

Name _____

Word Play

Match each word to its meaning.

| what engineers make to meet needs and solve problems | environment |

| all the living and nonliving things in a place | technology |

Write two ways technology can affect the environment.

_____

_____

_____

_____

Fill in the chart. Write different kinds
of technology.

Technology

Technology I Use Every Day
_____
_____

Technology I Must Use With Care
_____
_____

Technology That Affects the Environment
_____
_____

Take It Home!

Family Members: Ask your child to point out
examples of technology in your home. Discuss how
to use the technology safely.

Name _____

Essential Question

How Can We Improve Technology?

Set a Purpose

Tell what you want to find out.

_____

_____

Think About the Procedure

1 What are some objects you could choose?

_____

_____

2 How could you improve your object?

_____

Record Your Data

Draw to communicate your solution. Label your picture.

Draw Conclusions

How did your solution improve the object you chose?

_____

_____

_____

Ask More Questions

What other questions could you ask about improving technology?

_____

_____

_____

_____

Ask a Roller Coaster Designer

Now It's Your Turn!

▶ What question would you ask a roller coaster designer?

_____

_____

_____

_____

What do roller coaster designers do?
We design roller coasters for amusement parks. We think up ideas for new rides. We also figure out how much they will cost to build.

Do designers work alone?
We work as a team with engineers to make a design. The design has to work and be safe and fun for riders. A factory then builds the ride.

How long does it take to build a roller coaster?
It usually takes about a year from design to finish. A simpler design takes less time.

Design Your Own Roller Coaster

▶ Draw your own roller coaster in the space below.

▶ Explain your design. Write about how your roller coaster moves.

_____

_____

_____

Vocabulary Review

Use the terms in the box to complete the sentences.

> design process
> environment
> technology

1. A set of steps engineers follow to solve problems is a(n) _____.

2. What engineers make to meet needs and solve problems is _____.

3. All of the living and nonliving things in a place is a(n) _____.

Science Concepts

Fill in the letter of the choice that best answers the question.

4. What kind of work do engineers do?
   - Ⓐ make new designs for people to buy
   - Ⓑ invent new steps in the design process
   - Ⓒ solve problems using math and science

5. How can technology affect an environment?
   - Ⓐ It can help.
   - Ⓑ It can hurt.
   - Ⓒ It can help or hurt.

6. You chose these items to design a solution to a problem.

What step of the design process did you do?

Ⓐ Find a problem.

Ⓑ Plan and build.

Ⓒ Test and improve.

7. Which classroom object is an example of technology?

Ⓐ a pencil

Ⓑ a plant

Ⓒ a student

8. Why do engineers use the design process?

Ⓐ It is easy.

Ⓑ It helps them use tools.

Ⓒ It helps them solve problems.

9. Look at this object.

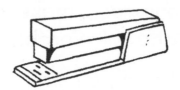

What is it an example of?

Ⓐ the design process

Ⓑ an engineer

Ⓒ technology

10. When do people use technology?

Ⓐ only when there is a problem

Ⓑ almost every day to meet their needs

Ⓒ only when they want to help the environment

11. You are following the steps in the design process. How can you tell whether a solution works?

Ⓐ Ask other people.

Ⓑ Draw and write about the solution.

Ⓒ Test the solution.

12. How is this person using technology?

Ⓐ to clean

Ⓑ to stay safe

Ⓒ to cook dinner

Inquiry and the Big Idea
Write the answers to these questions.

13. You need a way to carry six drink cans or bottles at the same time. Explain the steps you would follow to design a tool to solve your problem.

1. _____

2. _____

3. _____

4. _____

14. Look at the picture.

a. Identify how people use this technology.

_____

_____

b. What is good about this technology?

_____

c. What is bad about this technology?

_____

UNIT 3
Objects in the Sky

moon in the nighttime sky

Big Idea

The sun warms land, air, and water. The appearance of objects in the sky changes.

S2E1, S2E1.a, S2E1.b, S2E2, S2E2.a, S2E2.b, S2E2.c, S2E2.d

I Wonder Why
The moon looks lit in the nighttime sky. Why?
Turn the page to find out.

Here's Why The moon reflects light from the sun. This makes it look lit at nighttime.

In this unit, you will explore this Big Idea, the Essential Questions, and the Investigations on the Inquiry Flipchart.

Levels of Inquiry Key ■ DIRECTED ■ **GUIDED** ■ INDEPENDENT

Track Your Progress

Big Idea The sun warms land, air, and water. The appearance of objects in the sky changes.

Essential Questions

Now I Get the Big Idea!

Science Notebook

Before you begin each lesson, be sure to write your thoughts about the Essential Question.

S2E1.a Size and brightness of stars; **S2E1.b** Size and brightness of the sun.

Essential Question

What Can We See in the Sky?

Engage Your Brain!

Find the answer to the question in the lesson.

When can you see the moon?

_____

Active Reading

Lesson Vocabulary

1 Preview the lesson.

2 Write the five vocabulary terms here.

_____   _____

_____   _____

_____

Good Morning, Sunshine

sun

Look up! You can see many things in the daytime sky. You can see the sun. The **sun** is the star closest to Earth. A **star** is an object in the sky. It gives off its own light. The sun gives light and heat to Earth.

You may also see clouds in the daytime sky. Sometimes, you can even see the moon.

Active Reading

The main idea is the most important idea about something. Draw two lines under the main idea.

clouds

▶ What can you see in the daytime sky? Look out your window. Draw what you see.

Just an Average Star

The sun is the center of our solar system. Because it is the closest star to Earth, it is the biggest and brightest star we see.

But the sun is not the biggest and brightest star there is. There are many other stars, farther away from Earth, that are bigger and brighter than the sun. Some stars are smaller and not as bright as the sun.

Active Reading

The main idea is the most important idea about something. Draw two lines under the main idea.

Compared to other stars, the sun is a medium-sized star.

▶ Why don't you see many other stars in the sky during the daytime?

_____

_____

_____

Good Night, Sky

moon

You can see many things in the nighttime sky. You may see the moon. The **moon** is a large sphere, or ball of rock. It does not give off its own light. You may also see clouds at night.

Active Reading

Draw one line under a detail. Draw an arrow to the main idea it tells about.

© Houghton Mifflin Harcourt Publishing Company (bg) © John Lund/Getty Images

You may see stars in the nighttime sky. There are too many stars to count. They are not evenly spaced in the sky.

star

Do the Math!

Compare Solid Shapes

Many objects in the sky are spheres. A sphere is a round ball. The moon is a sphere. So is the sun. Color the spheres below.

Star Bright

What makes a star shine bright? Stars are made up of hot gases, which give off light.

There are many different types of stars. Some are 100 times bigger than the sun. Some older stars are smaller than Earth.

Active Reading

Find the sentence that tells why a star shines.

Stars are different sizes.

Most stars can only be seen at night. They look like tiny points of light because they are so far away. When you look at stars, can you tell if they are big or small?

red dwarf

our sun

blue-white supergaint

red giant

Star Sizes

▶Why are some stars brighter than other stars?

_____

_____

Eye on the Sky

Stars and other objects in the sky look small. We can magnify them to see them better. **Magnify** means to make something look bigger. A **telescope** is a tool that helps us magnify things in the sky.

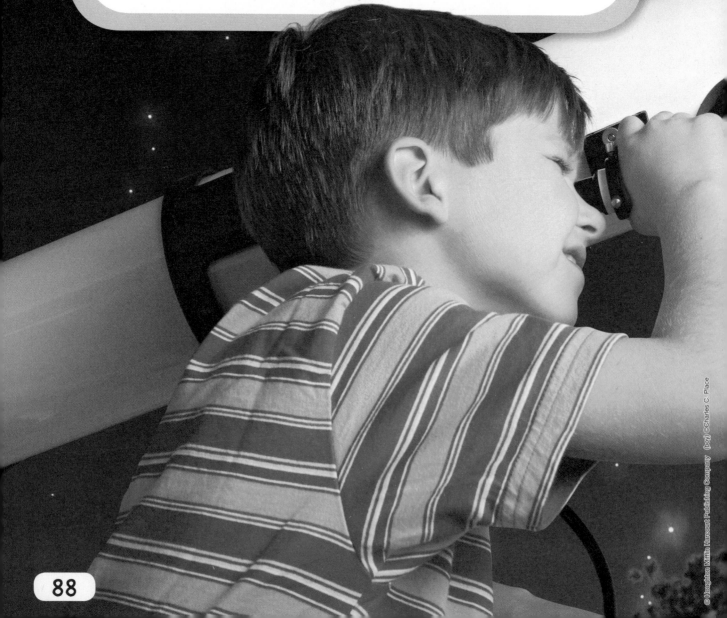

▶ Which picture shows the moon through a telescope? Mark an X on it.

telescope

Both pictures show the moon.

Sum It Up!

① Solve It!

Solve the riddle.

I am a tool. I make things look bigger. You can use me to observe things in the sky.

What am I?

_____

② Circle It!

Circle true or false.

Stars are evenly spaced in the sky.

true   false

Stars are different sizes and brightness.

true   false

③ Draw It!

Draw what you can see in the sky at both times.

daytime	nighttime

 **Brain Check**

Name _____

Word Play

Unscramble the letters to complete each sentence.

| sun | star | telescope | magnify | moon |

omon   The ___ ___ ___ ___ is a large ball of rock.

tasr   A ___ ___ ___ ___ gives off its own light.

eletopsce   A ___ ___ ___ ___ ___ ___ ___ ___ ___ is a tool for making things look bigger.

usn   The ___ ___ ___ is the star we see in the day.

fimgany   To ___ ___ ___ ___ ___ ___ ___ is to make things look bigger.

Apply Concepts

1 Fill in the diagram to compare.
Use the words below.

sun	stars	clouds	moon

daytime
sky

both

nighttime
sky

2 Draw a nighttime sky full of stars.

Family Members: See *ScienceSaurus*® for more
information about objects in the sky.

Take It
Home!

4 Things to Know About Galileo Galilei

1 Galileo lived in Italy more than 400 years ago.

2 His telescope made objects look 20 times bigger.

3 He discovered sunspots on the sun.

4 He found out that the planet Jupiter has four moons.

This Leads to That

Galileo used his telescope to observe the sun and planets.

He proved that Earth moves around the sun.

▶ People used to think that the sun moved around Earth. Galileo proved this was wrong. Why is this important?

_____

_____

_____

Name _____

What Can We Observe About the Moon?

Set a Purpose

Tell what you want to find out.

_____

_____

Think About the Procedure

1 When will you look at the moon?

_____

_____

2 What will you use to observe the moon?

_____

_____

Record Your Data

Write down what you observe about the moon in the chart.

My Observations of the Moon

	Shape	Brightness	Surface
Night 1			
Night 2			

Draw Conclusions

Why does the moon have dark and light spots?

_____

_____

Where does moonlight come from?

_____

_____

Ask More Questions

What other questions could you ask about the moon?

_____

_____

© Houghton Mifflin Harcourt Publishing Company

Essential Question

How Does the Sky Seem to Change?

Engage Your Brain!

Find the answer to the question in the lesson.

Why does the sun seem to move across the sky?

Earth _____.

Active Reading

Lesson Vocabulary

1 Preview the lesson.

2 Write the two vocabulary terms here.

_____   _____

Hello, Shadow

The sun is the brightest object in the daytime sky. It warms Earth's land, air, and water. The sun seems to move across the sky. But the sun is not moving. It is really Earth that is moving. Each day, Earth turns all the way around.

Active Reading

The main idea is the most important idea about something. Draw two lines under the main idea.

morning

Light from the sun makes shadows.
A **shadow** is a dark place made where an
object blocks light. Shadows change as
Earth moves. The sun's light shines on objects
from different directions as the day goes on.
Shadows change in size during the day.
They change position, too.

▶ At what time of day is the girl's
shadow the shortest?

_____

noon

afternoon

Make a Sundial

Billy and Jennifer head out to the backyard to begin their task. Billy puts a paper plate on the ground and inserts a pencil in the center. Jennifer uses a marker to draw numbers on the paper plate just like on a clock.

Active Reading

Find the sentence that explains what Billy used to make the sundial. Draw a line under the sentence.

Billy and Jennifer want to learn how shadows change during the day.

Jennifer observes the shadow of the pencil and circles the number on the paper plate where it falls. Billy and Jennifer come back 2 hours later and observe the shadow of the pencil again. Billy circles the number on the plate where it now falls.

▶ Look at the two pictures of the sundial. How did the shadow change?

_____

_____

Just a Phase

Now it is night. You may see stars. You may see the moon. The moon is a huge ball of rock. It does not give off its own light. The moon reflects light from the sun.

Active Reading

A detail is a fact about a main idea. Draw one line under a detail. Draw an arrow to the main idea it tells about.

new moon

first quarter moon

The moon moves across the sky. Its shape seems to change. The **phases**, or shapes you see, change as the moon moves. The changes follow a repeating pattern. It lasts about a month.

▶ Today there is a full moon. Write what the moon's phase will be in about a month.

_____

full moon

third quarter moon

Cloudy Day, Starry Night

You can see stars in the nighttime sky. Stars give off light. You see different stars in each season.

You can see clouds in both the daytime and nighttime sky. Clouds are always changing shape.

You may see these stars in summer.

You may see these stars in winter.

These kinds
of clouds may
bring rain.

These kinds of clouds
can be seen on a
sunny day.

▶ Draw a cloud that
might bring rain.

Sum It Up!

① Solve It!

Write the word to solve the riddle.

I am fluffy or thin.
I am white or gray.
I come out on
some days and then
go away.
I am a _____.

② Draw It!

Draw the boy's shadow in the morning.

③ Mark It!

Cross out the picture of the full moon. Put a box around the picture of the new moon.

106

Name _____

Word Play

Label each picture with a word from the box.
Match the word to its meaning.

sun	phases	shadow

_____

dark place made where an object blocks light

_____

shapes you see of the moon

_____

brightest object in the daytime sky

Apply Concepts

Write the words that tell more about each column. Each word may be used more than once.

| sun | clouds | stars | moon |

Daytime Sky	Nighttime Sky	Gives Off Its Own Light	Moves or Seems to Move
_____	_____	_____	_____
_____	_____	_____	_____
_____	_____		_____
			_____

Take It Home!

Family Members: Look at the moon with your child for a few nights in a row. Ask your child to describe how the moon seems to change shape.

Name _____

Essential Question

How Does the Sun Seem to Move?

Set a Purpose

Tell what you want to find out.

_____

_____

Think About the Procedure

1 When will you look at your shadow? Where will you stand?

_____

_____

2 How will you know how your shadow changes?

_____

_____

Record Your Data

Write the number of shoes in the chart.

My Shadow's Length

Morning	Noon	Afternoon
_____ shoes long	_____ shoes long	_____ shoes long

Draw Conclusions

How do you know your shadow changed?

_____

_____

How did your shadow change from morning to noon?

_____

How did it change from noon to afternoon?

_____

Ask More Questions

What other questions could you ask about shadows?

_____

_____

Essential Question

How Can We Recognize Changes in Seasons?

 Engage Your Brain!

Find the answer to the question in the lesson.

When might you see ice and snow on the ground?

You might see this in

_____.

Active Reading

Lesson Vocabulary

1 Preview the lesson.

2 Write the three vocabulary terms here.

_____   _____

_____

Season to Season

A **season** is a time of year that has a certain kind of weather. Weather changes each season. The seasons follow the same pattern every year.

Fabulous Fall

In fall the air outside may be cool. Leaves of some trees change color and drop off.

Wonderful Winter

Winter is the coldest season. Ice can form on land and plants. In some places snow may fall. Winter has the fewest hours of daylight.

▶ Which season comes after spring?

_____

Sunny Spring

In spring the air gets warmer. Some places get a lot of rain.

Super Summer

Summer is the warmest season. Some places have sudden storms. Summer has the most hours of daylight.

A Change of Pace

Changes in temperature, sunlight, and precipitation affect plants and animals, which can help us recognize changes in seasons.

▶ **How does rainfall and temperature affect plants?**

_____

_____

_____

fall

winter

spring

summer

There is cooler weather in fall. The leaves of some plants change color and drop off. By winter, the plants have lost their leaves. In spring, more rain and warmer weather cause new leaves to grow. Leaves keep growing in summer.

Less sunlight and cooler temperatures cause most plants to lose their leaves. The plants go through a period called dormancy. Dormancy is a time when plants stop growing. Most plants go through dormancy in winter.

Warm temperatures and precipitation can cause seeds in the ground to grow. We can recognize a change in seasons when seeds sprout up from the ground and begin to grow.

dormant tree

growing plants

Animals may migrate during some seasons. To migrate is to travel from one place to another and back again. Watering holes may dry up if there is no rainfall in a season. Some animals will migrate to a place where they can find water.

wildebeest at a watering hole

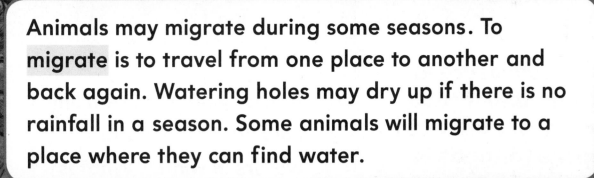

Sum It Up!

1 Match It!

Match the picture to the word that tells about it.

spring

winter

2 Circle It!

Circle the ways a tree can change with the seasons.

Its leaves drop off.

It migrates.

Its leaves change color.

3 Write It!

The temperature is warmer, and it rains more often. Tell what happens to seeds in the ground.

_____

_____

_____

4 Answer It!

A gray whale swims from cold waters to warm waters in winter. What is this an example of?

_____

Name _____

Word Play

Fill in the blanks. Use each word from the word bank.

dormancy	fall	season	migrate

Dear Aunt Lucy,

Thanks for letting me come see you. Summer is usually my favorite _____ to visit you. This time, I liked being there in _____ when the leaves were changing color.

Walking in the woods was great. It was the first time I saw birds starting to _____ to their winter homes. It was cool to learn that in the winter plants stop growing and go into _____.
I'll have to come in spring when they begin to start growing again!

Your nephew,

Ben

Apply Concepts

Fill in the chart. Show how we can recognize changes in seasons.

How We Recognize Changes in Seasons

Plants	Animals	Weather
_____	_____	_____
_____	_____	_____
_____	_____	_____
_____	_____	_____
_____	_____	_____
_____	_____	_____
_____	_____	_____
_____	_____	_____
_____	_____	_____

Take It Home!

Family Members: Ask your child to choose a favorite season. Then discuss how we can recognize changes in seasons.

See the Light

Compare Flashlights

Lights help you see what you are doing. They help you get around at night. The lights in a building make it bright.

Flashlights can light up dark places. Flashlights work in different ways.

- uses a switch
- needs batteries
- lights up right away

- uses a hand crank
- does not need batteries
- takes time to light up

Bright Ideas

Think about a kind of light, like a lamp. How can you make it better? Draw your design. Tell how your design works.

_____

_____

Build On It!

Design lights for a ballpark. Complete **Design It: Lights for a Park** on the Inquiry Flipchart.

Name _____

Vocabulary Review

Use the terms in the box to complete the sentences.

| phases |
| shadow |
| star |

1. An object in the sky that gives off its own light is a

   _____.

2. A dark place made where an object blocks light is a

   _____.

3. The shapes of the moon you see as it moves are its

   _____.

Science Concepts

Fill in the letter of the choice that best answers the question.

4. How many stars are in the sky?
   Ⓐ about 20
   Ⓑ not enough to be counted
   Ⓒ more than anyone can easily count

5. What objects can we see in the nighttime sky?
   Ⓐ the sun and clouds
   Ⓑ the moon and stars
   Ⓒ the sun and the moon

6. What heats Earth's land, water, and air?

   Ⓐ clouds

   Ⓑ the moon

   Ⓒ the sun

7. What moon phase does this picture show?

   Ⓐ full moon

   Ⓑ new moon

   Ⓒ first quarter moon

8. Compared to all other stars, the sun is what size?

   Ⓐ small

   Ⓑ medium

   Ⓒ large

9. Which happens because Earth turns?

   Ⓐ The sun warms Earth.

   Ⓑ The moon has phases.

   Ⓒ The sun seems to move across the sky.

10. How do stars look in the nighttime sky?

    Ⓐ They are scattered unevenly.

    Ⓑ They are set in a pattern of rings.

    Ⓒ They are set evenly across the sky.

11. How do you know a season is changing?

    Ⓐ when seeds begin to grow

    Ⓑ when birds begin to fly

    Ⓒ when clouds cover the sun

12. Which picture shows the flag at the end of the day?

Ⓐ the picture with the long shadow

Ⓑ the picture with the short shadow

Ⓒ both pictures

13. Yoon sees different stars on a winter night than he sees on a summer night. Why?

Ⓐ You can see stars only in the winter sky.

Ⓑ Clouds may block the stars in summer.

Ⓒ You can see different stars in different seasons.

14. In which season do leaves change colors?

Ⓐ summer

Ⓑ fall

Ⓒ winter

Inquiry and the Big Idea

Write the answers to these questions.

15. You want to get a closer look at the stars in the sky.

a. What tool can help you see the stars better?

_____

b. How does this tool help you?

_____

_____

16. Compare and contrast the stars and the moon.

a. What is one way they are the same?

_____

_____

b. Name a way they are different.

_____

_____

_____

Plants and Animals

Big Idea

All plants and animals grow and change. They have life cycles.

S2L1, S2L1.a, S2L1.b, S2L1.d

hummingbird and flower

I Wonder Why

Hummingbirds are attracted to certain flowers. Why?

Turn the page to find out.

Here's Why Many brightly colored flowers with tube-like shapes hold the most nectar. Hummingbirds eat nectar to grow and live.

In this unit, you will explore this Big Idea, the Essential Questions, and the Investigations on the Inquiry Flipchart.

Levels of Inquiry Key ■ DIRECTED ■ GUIDED ■ INDEPENDENT

Track Your Progress

Big Idea All plants and animals grow and change. They have life cycles.

Essential Questions

Now I Get the Big Idea!

Science Notebook

Before you begin each lesson, be sure to write your thoughts about the Essential Question.

Essential Question

What Are Some Animal Life Cycles?

 Engage Your Brain!

Find the answer to the riddle in this lesson.

When is a frog not like a frog?

When it is

a _____ .

Active Reading

Lesson Vocabulary

1 Preview the lesson.

2 Write the six vocabulary terms here.

_____   _____

_____   _____

_____   _____

Animal Start-Ups

A dog can have puppies. A cat can have kittens. Adult animals can **reproduce**, or have young. Animals such as puppies and kittens look like their parents. How does a kitten look like an adult cat?

Other young animals look very different from their parents. They go through changes and become like their parents.

A young butterfly does not look like its parents.

A young cat looks like its parents.

▶ Name another animal that looks like its parents.

_____

What's in the Egg?

Many animals begin life by hatching from an egg. Animals change as they grow. The changes that happen to an animal during its life make up its **life cycle**.

▶ How are the animals in this chart alike?

_____

_____

Animal Life Cycles

Kind of Animal	Egg	Young	Adult
Chicken			
Turtle			
Rainbow Trout			

1

2

Egg

A frog begins life inside a tiny egg.

Young Tadpole

A **tadpole** hatches from the egg. It lives in water. It takes in oxygen with gills.

Hatch, Swim, Hop

Did you know that a frog begins life inside a tiny egg? The young frog goes through changes to become an adult. These changes are called **metamorphosis**.

Growing Tadpole

The tadpole gets bigger. It grows four legs. Later, it loses its tail.

Frog

The adult can live on land or in the water. It hops. It breathes with lungs.

Polar Parenting

It is late October. A female polar bear gets a shelter ready for her cubs. She digs a den in the snow. The den will keep her young warm and safe. She gives birth in winter.

▶ **How is a polar bear's life cycle different from a frog's life cycle?**

_____

Newborn

A polar bear cub is born inside the den. It drinks milk from its mother's body.

Growing Cub

The cub begins to explore outside the den.

We'll stay with our mother for almost three years, until we're grown up.

3

4

Young Polar Bear

The young polar bear learns to swim and hunt.

Adult Polar Bear

The adult polar bear can live on its own. It can have its own young.

The Mighty Monarch

A monarch butterfly has a life cycle, too. An adult female butterfly lays a tiny egg. The egg is so small it is hard to see. This picture shows a close-up of an egg on a leaf.

1 egg

▶ Why do you think a butterfly egg is so small?

_____

_____

2 larva

A tiny **larva**, or caterpillar, hatches from the egg. A caterpillar is a young butterfly. The larva eats a lot and grows quickly.

Then the larva stops eating and moving. The larva becomes a pupa. It makes a hard covering.

A **pupa** goes through metamorphosis inside the covering. It grows wings. Many other changes also happen.

3 pupa

4 adult

Finally, an adult butterfly comes out of the covering. It can have its own young.

Active Reading

Clue words can help you find the order of events. Draw a box around the clue words **then** and **finally**.

Sum It Up!

① Mark It!

Draw an X on the animal that does not look like its young.

② Draw It!

Draw a picture of this animal's mother.

③ Solve It!

Answer the riddle.

I am little now.
I will change and grow.
Someday I will be an adult cat.
What am I? _____

④ Think About It!

Is a 👶 most like a 🐻 , a 🦎 , or a 🐛 ? Why?

Name _____

Word Play

Use these words to complete the puzzle.

tadpole   change   pupa   larva   reproduce   cycle

Across

1. The stage in a butterfly's life cycle after the egg

2. To make more living things of the same kind

Down

3. The stage in a butterfly's life between larva and adult

4. A young frog that lives in water

5. This takes place during metamorphosis in frogs and butterflies

6. All the stages of an animal's life make up its life _____.

Apply Concepts

How is the life cycle of a butterfly different from the life cycle of a polar bear? Use this chart to show your answer.

Life Cycles

Butterfly	Polar Bear
A butterfly hatches from an egg.	_____ _____
_____ _____	A polar bear cub drinks milk from its mother's body.
_____ _____	A polar bear cub looks a lot like its parents.
A butterfly larva does not stay with its parents.	_____ _____

Take It Home!

Family Members: Discuss life cycles with your child. Sort family photographs to show ways that your child and others have grown and changed over the years.

Essential Question

What Are Some Plant Life Cycles?

Engage Your Brain!

Find the answer to the question in this lesson.

What does the flower part of a dandelion make?

It makes

_____.

Active Reading

Lesson Vocabulary

1 Preview the lesson.

2 Write the four vocabulary terms here.

_____   _____

_____   _____

Plant Start-Ups

Plants are living things. They grow and change. They have life cycles. Most plant life cycles begin with a **seed**. New plants grow from seeds. The growing plants start to look like their parent plants.

Active Reading

Find the words that tell about seeds. Draw a line under the words.

The plants in this garden grew from seeds.

How Fast Do Plants Grow?

Some plants grow quickly. Plants in a vegetable garden take just a few months to become adult plants. Other plants, such as trees, take many years to become adults.

Do the Math!
Interpret a Table

Use the chart to answer the question.

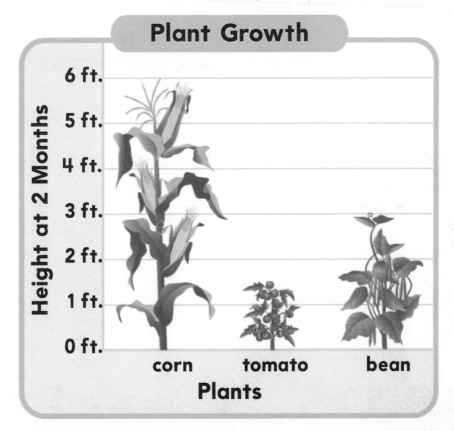

Plant Growth

▶ How much taller did the corn plant grow than the bean plant?

Start with a Seed

What happens when you plant a seed? When a seed gets warmth, air, and water, it may germinate. **Germinate** means to start to grow. The stem of the tiny plant breaks through the ground. The plant gets taller and grows leaves.

▶ Which plant parts grow from the seed first?

_____

A tiny plant is inside a seed.

The seed germinates. The roots grow down.

The stem grows up toward the light.

Growing Up

The tiny plant inside the seed has become a young plant called a **seedling**.

The seedling grows into an adult plant. An adult plant can make flowers and seeds.

Active Reading

Find the words that tell the meaning of **seedling**. Draw a line under those words.

The plant grows more roots and leaves.

The adult plant grows flowers.

Apples
All Around

Some plants have flowers that make seeds and fruit. Parts of the flower grow into fruit. The fruit grows around the seeds to hold and protect them.

Active Reading

Circle the word **seeds** each time you see it on these two pages.

apple blossoms

Parts of apple blossoms grow into apples. The apples grow around seeds.

A Long Life

Some plants have short lives. They die soon after their flowers make seeds. Other plants, such as apple trees, can live for many years. An apple tree can live for a hundred years or more!

adult apple tree

► **What do apple blossoms make?**

Inside a Cone

Some plants, like pine trees, do not have flowers. But they do have seeds. Where do their seeds grow? A **cone** is a part of a pine tree and some other plants. Seeds grow inside the cone.

closed pinecones

open pinecones with seeds

The cone protects the seeds until they are ready to germinate. Then the cone opens up, and the seeds can fall out.

▶ Where do pine seeds form?

Pine Tree Beginnings

Pine seeds fall to the ground and germinate. As the seedlings grow, they start to look like their parent plants. After a few years, the pine trees grow cones and make seeds. The life cycle begins again.

adult pine trees

▶ **What happens after an adult pine tree grows cones and makes seeds?**

_____

_____

Sum It Up!

① Draw It!

Draw the missing step in the plant's life cycle.
Label your picture.

seed   _____   seedling   adult

② Mark It!

Draw an X on the plant part that does not have seeds.

③ Think About It!

How are flowers and pinecones alike?

_____

_____

Name _____

Word Play

Read each word. Trace a path through the maze to connect each word to its picture.

seed	cone	flower	seedling

Apply Concepts

Write to tell about the life cycle of a plant. Use the words <u>germinate</u>, <u>seed</u>, and <u>seedling</u>.

Life Cycle of a Plant

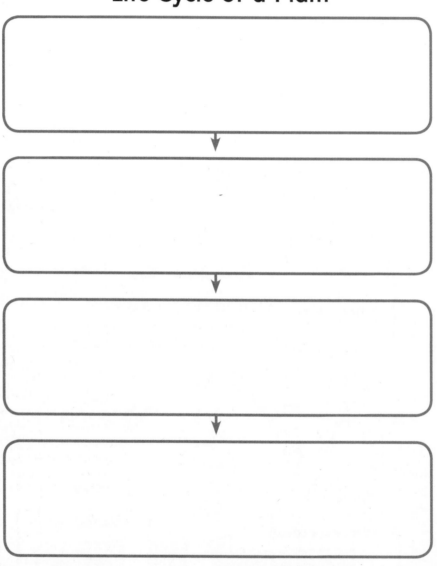

© Houghton Mifflin Harcourt Publishing Company

Get to Know...

Dr. Maria Elena Zavala

As a young girl, Maria Elena Zavala thought a lot about plants. Her grandmother lived next door. She grew plants to use as medicine. Young Maria learned about those plants from her grandmother.

Today Maria Elena Zavala is a botanist and a teacher. A botanist is a scientist who studies plants. Dr. Zavala studies how plants respond to their environment. She and her students are finding out how roots grow.

Fun Fact

As a child, Maria took apart her father's roses to learn more about plants.

Now You Be a Botanist!

▶ Draw and label roots, flowers, and leaves on this plant.

Name _____

Essential Question

How Does a Bean Plant Grow?

Set a Purpose

Explain what you will learn from this activity.

_____

_____

Think About the Procedure

❶ Why must you give the plant water and sunlight?

_____

_____

❷ Compare the way that your bean plant grew with the way that a classmate's bean plant grew. What was the same?

_____

_____

_____

Record Your Data

In this chart, record what you observe.

Date	Observations

Draw Conclusions

How did the bean plant change?

_____

_____

_____

Ask More Questions

What other questions could you ask about how plants grow?

_____

_____

Bringing Water to Plants

Drip Irrigation

Irrigation is a way to get water to land so plants can grow. A lawn sprinkler is one kind of irrigation.

Drip irrigation is another kind of irrigation. Hoses carry water to plants. Water drips from emitters on the hoses. This brings water right to the soil around the plants. Less water is wasted. Less water evaporates.

emitter

hose

Two Ways

Compare sprinkler irrigation and drip irrigation. Write a possible good thing and bad thing about each system.

Good _____

_____

Bad _____

_____

Good _____

_____

Bad _____

_____

Build On It!

Compare different kinds of drip irrigation. Complete **Compare It: Drip Tips** on the Inquiry Flipchart.

Unit 4 Review

Vocabulary Review

Use the terms in the box to complete the sentences.

| germinate |
| metamorphosis |
| reproduce |
| seed |

1. When adult animals have young animals, they _____.

2. The changes an animal goes through are called _____.

3. Most plants grow from a _____.

4. When a seed gets warmth, air, and water, it may _____.

Science Concepts

Fill in the letter of the choice that best answers the question.

5. How is a frog's life cycle the same as a bird's life cycle?
   - Ⓐ Both hatch from an egg.
   - Ⓑ Both go through metamorphosis.
   - Ⓒ Both look like their parents when they are born.

6. When do polar bears give birth?
   - Ⓐ summer
   - Ⓑ winter
   - Ⓒ all year long

7. Where does a frog begin life?

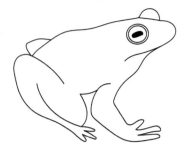

Ⓐ in the ocean
Ⓑ inside an egg
Ⓒ inside a pupa

8. What does a pupa become after it goes through metamorphosis?
Ⓐ an adult butterfly
Ⓑ a larva
Ⓒ a caterpillar

9. This bird is hatching from an egg.

Which animal's life cycle is **most** similar to the bird's life cycle?
Ⓐ a bear
Ⓑ a dog
Ⓒ a turtle

10. Which plant part makes seeds?

Ⓐ flower
Ⓑ leaves
Ⓒ roots

11. Which part of the plant life cycle does this picture show?

Ⓐ adult plant
Ⓑ seed
Ⓒ seedling

12. How do you know that this plant is an adult plant?

Ⓐ The plant has roots.
Ⓑ The plant has leaves.
Ⓒ The plant has a flower.

13. What does a cone do?
Ⓐ A cone grows fruit.
Ⓑ A cone holds seeds.
Ⓒ A cone makes pollen.

Inquiry and the Big Idea

Write the answers to these questions.

14. What are the four stages in the life cycle of this animal?

Stage 1 _____

Stage 2 _____

Stage 3 _____

Stage 4 _____

15. Tell how you would plan an investigation to show that plants need water to survive.

_____

_____

_____

Environments for Living Things

impala and red-billed oxpecker

Big Idea

Living things meet their needs in their environments.

S2E3, S2E3.a, S2E3.b, S2L1, S2L1.c

I Wonder Why

The bird is picking bugs off the impala. Why?
Turn the page to find out.

Here's Why The bird eats the bugs for food.

In this unit, you will explore this Big Idea, the Essential Questions, and the Investigations on the Inquiry Flipchart.

Levels of Inquiry Key ■ DIRECTED ■ **GUIDED** ■ INDEPENDENT

Track Your Progress

Big Idea Living things meet their needs in their environments.

Essential Questions

Now I Get the Big Idea!

Science Notebook

Before you begin each lesson, be sure to write your thoughts about the Essential Question.

Essential Question

How Do Plants and Animals Need One Another?

Engage Your Brain!

Find the answer to the question in the lesson.

This bat drinks from the plant. How is the bat also helping the plant?

The bat spreads

_____ .

Active Reading

Lesson Vocabulary

1. Preview the lesson.

2. Write the three vocabulary terms here.

_____ _____

_____

In Your Place

Plants and animals use living and nonliving things to meet their needs. They get the things they need from their environment. All the living and nonliving things in a place make up an **environment**.

Active Reading

Find the sentence that tells the meaning of **environment**. Draw a line under the sentence.

Plants and animals need water.

Plants and animals need air.

Plants need sunlight to make food. Animals find food in their environment.

Plants and animals need space to live and grow. Animals find shelter in the environment where they live.

▶ What do both plants and animals need from their environment?

_____

_____

Getting Help

Animals use plants to meet their needs. Many animals use plants for shelter. Some animals hide in plants. Other animals live in plants or use them to build homes.

Active Reading

A detail is a fact about a main idea. Draw one line under a detail. Draw an arrow to the main idea it tells about.

An owl finds shelter in a tree.

A lion hides in tall grass.

Animals need to breathe air to get oxygen, a gas in the air. Plants give off oxygen. Some animals use plants for food. Some animals eat animals that eat plants.

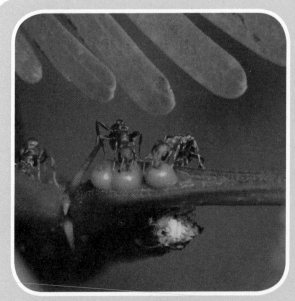

Ants find both food and shelter in the thorns of this tree.

A panda eats bamboo.

▶ Write another example of how an animal uses plants to meet its needs.

_____

_____

_____

_____

Giving Help

Animals may help plants reproduce, or make new plants. Some animals carry fruits to new places. There, the seeds inside the fruits may grow into new plants.

The dog spreads seeds that are inside the burrs on its fur.

Some animals spread pollen for plants. **Pollen** is a powder that flowers need to make seeds. Pollen may stick to an animal. The animal carries the pollen from flower to flower. This helps plants make new plants.

As a bat drinks the flower nectar, pollen rubs off on the bat.

A woodpecker moves acorns with its beak. Seeds are inside the acorns.

A beetle carries pollen on its body.

▶ Underline two examples of how animals help plants reproduce.

169

Eat Up!

These pictures show a food chain.
A **food chain** shows how energy moves from
plants to animals. Follow the arrows. They show
how plants and animals are linked in a
food chain.

Food chains start with sunlight and plants. In
this food chain, the water plants use sunlight
to make food.

An eagle eats the turtle.

A turtle eats the water plants.

▶ Draw what is missing from the first step of the food chain.

Sum It Up!

① Label It!

Write water, food, or shelter to tell what each living thing is getting from its environment.

_____   _____   _____   _____

② Order It!

Number the steps in this food chain to show the correct order.

_____   _____   _____

Name _____

Word Play

Read each clue below. Then unscramble the letters to write the correct answer.

| environment | oxygen | pollen | food chain |

1. a gas in the air that animals need to survive

   nxyego _____

2. all the living and nonliving things in a place

   nervnitnmeo _____

3. shows how energy moves from plants to animals

   ofod   inhca _____

4. flowers need this to make seeds

   lonpel _____

Use words from the word bank to complete the chart.

| shelter | oxygen | seeds | food | pollen |

Ways Animals Use Plants	Ways Animals Help Plants
When animals build nests, they use plants for _____.	Animals help carry _____ to new places.
Animals eat plants as _____.	Animals spread _____ that sticks to their bodies.
Animals need _____ that plants give off.	

Take It Home!

Family Members: See *ScienceSaurus®* for more information about environments.

Essential Question

How Are Living Things Adapted to Their Environments?

Engage Your Brain!

Find the answer to the question in the lesson.

Find the caterpillar. How do its color and shape help it stay safe?

They help it

_____

Active Reading

Lesson Vocabulary

1 Preview the lesson.

2 Write the vocabulary term here.

_____

Survival Skills

Plants live almost everywhere. Some places they live are dry. Other places are wet and shady. Plants have ways to survive where they live. These ways are called adaptations. An **adaptation** is something that helps a living thing survive in its environment.

Water lilies have long stems that let their leaves reach the water's surface. There, the leaves get sunlight.

▶ Look at this plant. Circle the kind of environment where it would best survive.

dry   wet

Cacti live where it is dry. Their thick, waxy stems store water.

Rain forest plants have very large leaves. These leaves help the plants get sunlight in the shady forest.

Animals At Home

Animals also have adaptations to help them survive in their environments. They may live where there is little food. They may live where it is very cold. Their adaptations help them survive where they live.

Active Reading

The main idea is the most important idea about something. Draw two lines under the main idea.

Camels live where it is dry and sandy. Long eyelashes help keep sand out of their eyes.

Penguins live on ice and in cold water. A thick layer of fat keeps them warm.

Giraffes have long tongues to pull leaves off trees.

▶ Look at this animal. Circle the kind of environment where it would best survive.

dry, sandy

cold water

Plant Protection

Living things also have adaptations to protect themselves. Plant adaptations help keep plants safe from animals that might eat them. Some of these adaptations are thorns, bad taste, and quick movement.

Daffodils taste bad. Animals do not like to eat them.

The thorns on a prickly pear cactus make it hard for animals to eat its fruit.

The leaves of the mimosa plant fold quickly when touched. This may knock off insects that want to eat the leaves.

▶ Name two plant adaptations that protect plants from animals.

_____

_____

_____

_____

Animal Protection

Many animals must protect themselves from other animals. They have adaptations to help them stay safe. These adaptations help protect animals from other animals that want to eat them.

Skunks can spray a bad smell. The bad smell scares off other animals.

© Houghton Mifflin Harcourt Publishing Company (b) ©Comstock/Stockbyte/Getty Images; (inset) ©Jeff Rotman/Getty Images

Sea urchins have long, sharp spines. The spines protect them from fish and crabs.

▶ Write two characteristics that help the leaf insect survive.

_____

_____

The leaf insect looks like the leaf. This helps the insect hide.

Sum It Up!

① Match It!

Match each living thing to the environment where it lives.

cold, snowy   dry, sandy   wet, shady

② Write It!

Write how each living thing protects itself.

_____   _____   _____

Name _____

Word Play

Define the word **adaptation**. Then list
adaptations that help plants and animals survive.

adaptation:

_____

_____

Plants	Animals
large leaves	fat
_____	_____
_____	_____
_____	_____
_____	_____
_____	_____

Apply Concepts

Write two details that go with the main idea.
Include details about two different adaptations.

Main Idea
Adaptations help living things survive in different environments.

Detail	Detail

Take It Home!

Family Members: Ask your child to describe some animal adaptations. Discuss how those adaptations help the animals survive.

Name _____

Can Plants Survive in Different Environments?

Set a Purpose

Write what you want to find out.

_____

Make a Prediction

Write a prediction about what you think will happen.

_____

_____

Think About the Procedure

1 Why will you water the **desert** plant only once?

_____

2 Why will you water the **rain forest** plant three times a day?

_____

Record Your Data

In this chart, record what you observe.

Date	Desert Plant	Rain Forest Plant

Draw Conclusions

Was your prediction right? Can a plant from one environment live in a different environment? How do you know?

_____

_____

Ask More Questions

What other questions could you ask about plants in different environments?

_____

_____

Technology and the Environment

Dams

A dam is a wall built across a river. It slows the flow of the river. A dam can be helpful. It can provide water for drinking. It can provide water for crops. It can also control floods.

A dam can also harm the environment. Fish, like salmon, cannot migrate across some dams. Some animals lose their homes when a dam is built.

salmon migrating

S.T.E.M.
continued

Helpful and Harmful

How are dams helpful? How are dams harmful? Use your ideas to complete the chart.

Effects of Dams	
Helpful	**Harmful**
_____	_____
_____	_____
_____	_____
_____	_____
_____	_____
_____	_____

Build On It!

Learn more about water and technology. Complete **Design It: Water Filter** on the Inquiry Flipchart.

Essential Question

How Do Environments Change Over Time?

Engage Your Brain!

Find the answer to the question in the lesson.

What changed this environment?

_____

Active Reading

Lesson Vocabulary

1 Preview the lesson.

2 Write the vocabulary term here.

_____

Nature's Work

Things happen in nature that can change environments over time. Different kinds of weather change an environment from season to season. Fires and earthquakes can make changes in minutes.

forest before a fire

Fire can change an environment. It burns trees and plants. Some animals move to safer places. Some animals may die.

The changes do not last forever. New trees and plants grow back. Animals come back to the area to live in the trees and eat the plants.

Active Reading

A cause tells why something happens. Draw one line under a cause.

forest during a fire

▶ Name an effect of fire on an environment.

_____

_____

A Change of Pace

Animals and plants can change an environment. The kudzu plant grows very fast. The plant will grow over other plants. The plants that are covered do not get enough light. They may die.

Beavers build dams, which form ponds. Beavers pile sticks, branches, and mud over a shallow area of running water. The dam blocks the running water and makes a pond.

When beavers cut down trees, some birds and insects lose their homes.

A kudzu plant has grown over these cars.

The pond that beavers make becomes a home for some plants and animals.

Do the Math!

Skip Count by 10s

A beaver dam can be 10 feet high! How high would 3 beaver dams be? Skip count to find the answer. Show your work.

_____ feet

What People Do

People change environments, too. People change environments because they need resources. A **resource** is anything people can use to meet their needs. People can help and harm environments. How do you change your environment?

Active Reading

Find the sentence that tells the meaning of **resource**. Draw a line under the sentence.

Pollution and trash harm environments.

Reducing trash and recycling help keep environments clean.

People may need to
cut down trees to make
space for buildings.

People help by
planting new trees.

▶ Write how people
can change the
environment.

help	harm

Sum It Up!

1 Match It!

Match each thing to the way it changes its environment.

burns trees

grows over
other plants

builds dams

2 Circle It!

Circle the ways that people can help an environment.

recycle   waste resources   plant trees

Brain Check

Name _____

Word Play

Draw lines to match each word to its description.

beaver   resource   recycle   kudzu

anything people can use to meet their needs

an animal that builds dams

a plant that grows over other plants

to use old resources to make new things

Apply Concepts

Fill in the chart. Write how each thing can change its environment.

How Environments Change

Things That Change Environments	How They Change Environments
fire	_____ _____
kudzu	_____ _____
beaver	_____ _____
people	_____ _____

Family Members: Walk with your child through your neighborhood. Observe and discuss ways that living things and other things that happen in nature have changed the environment.

Ask an Environmental Scientist

What do environmental scientists do?

We study the harmful effects to different kinds of environments.

How do environmental scientists help wildlife?

We find problems that affect wildlife and people in the environments. We figure out ways to solve those problems.

Sometimes people can harm an environment. For example, a factory may put waste into a stream. This may kill fish. We help the factory find other ways to get rid of its waste.

Now It's Your Turn!

▶ What question would you ask an environmental scientist?

_____

_____

_____

Making Environments Better

▶ Draw or write the answer to each question.

1 What do you think is most interesting about what environmental scientists do?

2 What might be difficult about what they do?

3 Why are environmental scientists important?

4 Think about being an environmental scientist. Draw an environment you would like to study.

Unit 5 Review

Vocabulary Review

Use the terms in the box to complete the sentences.

| adaptation |
| food chain |
| resource |

1. A(n) _____ shows how energy moves from plants to animals.

2. Anything that people can use to meet their needs is a(n) _____.

3. Humps help camels survive in their environment. Humps are a(n) _____.

Science Concepts

Fill in the letter of the choice that best answers the question.

4. Which is an example of a natural event changing a forest?
   - (A) a forest fire
   - (B) people planting trees
   - (C) people cutting down trees

5. How are the needs of plants and animals alike?
   - (A) Animals and plants both need sunlight to make their own food.
   - (B) Animals and plants both need air and water to survive.
   - (C) Animals and plants both need lungs to breathe.

6. This picture shows the steps in a food chain.

Which statement about this food chain is **true**?

Ⓐ Frogs eat grasshoppers.

Ⓑ Grasshoppers eat frogs.

Ⓒ Frogs and grasshoppers eat each other.

7. A plant has adaptations for living in a wet, shady environment. What will **most likely** happen if it is moved to a sunny, dry place?

Ⓐ The plant will die.

Ⓑ The plant will grow better.

Ⓒ The plant will grow as well.

8. What is the main reason people make changes to environments?

Ⓐ They need resources.

Ⓑ They have bad adaptations.

Ⓒ They want to help the environment.

9. Which begins every food chain?

Ⓐ plants

Ⓑ turtles

Ⓒ sunlight and plants

10. How do animals help plants meet their needs?

Ⓐ by making food for them

Ⓑ by spreading their seeds and pollen

Ⓒ by giving them shelter and oxygen

11. Look at the adaptations of this polar bear.

Where would the bear best survive?

Ⓐ hot, dry environment

Ⓑ cold, icy environment

Ⓒ warm, wet environment

12. Plants may change an environment over time. Which of these things can **most** change an environment in minutes?

Ⓐ animals

Ⓑ fire

Ⓒ soil

Inquiry and the Big Idea
Write the answers to these questions.

13. Describe two adaptations that would help an animal survive in a cold environment. Explain your answer.

_____

_____

14. Suppose a fire changes an environment. How will you know if a plant living in the environment has the adaptations to survive in the new environment?

_____

_____

_____

Changes in Matter

Big Idea

Matter can have different properties. Matter can be a solid, a liquid, or a gas. Properties of matter can change.

S2P1, S2P1.a, S2P1.b, S2P1.c

I Wonder Why

The floaties and the swim toys all keep their different shapes. Why?
Turn the page to find out.

Here's Why Gases take the shape of their container. This makes each object look different.

In this unit, you will explore this Big Idea, the Essential Questions, and the Investigations on the Inquiry Flipchart.

Levels of Inquiry Key ■ DIRECTED ■ **GUIDED** ■ INDEPENDENT

Big Idea Matter can have different properties. Matter can be a solid, a liquid, or a gas. Properties of matter can change.

Essential Questions

○ **Now I Get the Big Idea!**

Science Notebook

Before you begin each lesson, be sure to write your thoughts about the Essential Question.

Essential Question

What Is Matter?

Engage Your Brain!

Find the answer to the question in the lesson.

What is inside the balloon?

_____

Active Reading

Lesson Vocabulary

1 Preview the lesson.

2 Write the eight vocabulary terms here.

_____ _____

_____ _____

_____ _____

_____ _____

Matter Matters

The girl and the objects around her are matter. **Matter** is anything that takes up space and has mass. **Mass** is the amount of matter in an object.

Matter has properties. A **property** is one part of what something is like. Some properties are color, shape, size, and texture.

Active Reading

Find the sentence that tells the meaning of **mass**. Draw a line under the sentence.

Properties of Matter

▶ Look at the objects in each row. Draw something that has the same property.

---

color

---

shape

---

size

---

texture

State of the Art

Solid, liquid, and gas are three states of matter. The boy's sunglasses are a solid. The water in his bottle is a liquid. The beach ball is filled with gases.

Active Reading

The main idea is the most important idea about something. Draw two lines under the main idea.

What two states of matter make up the beach ball?

Solid as a Rock

Look at the chair, the towel, and the hat. How are these objects the same? The answer is that all three are solids.

A **solid** is the only state of matter that has its own shape. You can measure the mass of a solid. What other solids do you see in this picture?

▶ Draw a solid object that you would take to the beach.

Shape Up!

Is juice a solid? No. It does not have its own shape. If you pour juice from a pitcher into a glass, the shape of the juice changes.

Juice is a liquid. A **liquid** is a state of matter that takes the shape of its container. You can measure the volume of a liquid. **Volume** is the amount of space that matter takes up.

▶ Compare the pitcher to the glass on its right. Which container has the larger volume?

_____

Salt water is a kind of liquid.

Life's a Gas

This girl is blowing air into the beach ball. Air is made up of gases. A **gas** is a state of matter that fills all the space in its container. The air will keep spreading out until it fills the entire beach ball.

Active Reading

Find the sentence that tells the meaning of **gas**. Draw a line under the sentence.

You can't see air, but you can see and feel what it does.

Wonderful Water

On the outside of this glass, water vapor is becoming liquid water.

You can't see it, but water vapor is in the air around this glass.

There are three states of water—solid, liquid, and gas. The water we drink is a liquid. Solid water is ice. Water in the form of a gas is **water vapor**.

▶ What is water vapor?

_____

_____

States of Water

Write in each empty box to complete the chart.

Name	State	Shape
ice	solid	_____
water	_____	takes the shape of its container
_____	gas	fills up all the space in a container

Sum It Up!

① Match It!

Draw lines to match each object with its state of matter.

solid

liquid

gas

② Write It!

Answer the question.

What are the three states of water?

_____

_____

_____

③ Mark It!

Sort by properties. Draw an X on the object in each group that does <u>not</u> belong.

Name _____

Word Play

Write the word for each clue. Fill in the missing numbers in the table. Then decode the message.

a	b	c	d	e	f	g	h	i	j	k	l	m
	26	4		8	25		13		6	14		

n	o	p	q	r	s	t	u	v	w	x	y	z
7						17			10	5	12	24

takes the shape of its container

__ __ __ __ __ __
20 23   3   2   23   16

water in the form of a gas

__ __ __ __ __
15   11   1   18   22

amount of matter in an object

__ __ __ __
19   11   21   21

fills all the space of its container

__ __ __
9   11   21

__   __ __ __   __ __   __ __ __
11   16 11 12   11 17   17 13 8

__ __ __ __ __   __ __   __
26 8 11 4 13   23 21   11

__ __ __ __ __ __ __ __   __ __ __ __ __ __!
20 11 2 9 13 23 7 9   19 11 17 17 8 22

Apply Concepts

Write or draw to fill in the chart with examples of solids, liquids, and gases.

Solids, Liquids, and Gases

Solids	Liquids	Gases

Family Members: See *ScienceSaurus*® for more information about matter.

Take It Home!

Name _____

Essential Question

How Can New Structures Be Made?

Set a Purpose

Write what you will do in this investigation.

_____

State Your Hypothesis

Write your hypothesis, or the statement that you will test.

_____

_____

Think About the Procedure

How will you figure out what structures can be made?

_____

_____

_____

Record Your Data

Draw each of your structures in the chart.

Structure 1	Structure 3
Structure 2	Structure 4

Draw Conclusions

1 How were your structures the same? How were they different?

_____

_____

2 What can you do with structures that are made from small pieces?

_____

_____

Ask More Questions

What other questions can you ask about volume?

_____

_____

Kitchen Technology

Cooking Tools

The tools you use to cook are technology. They are designed to help you in the kitchen! A spoon is technology. So is an oven.

Whole Wheat Chocolate Chip Cookies

2 cups whole wheat flour
1 egg
1 teaspoon vanilla
1 teaspoon baking soda

A recipe tells you how to make food.

Measuring cups and spoons use standard units to measure ingredients.

A timer tells you when something has finished baking.

Make Do

Write to tell how you would solve
each problem.

1. You are baking muffins. The timer on your oven
is broken! How else could you measure how long
to bake the muffins?

_____

_____

2. You need 3 cups of flour for a recipe. You only
have a 1-cup measuring cup. How could you use it
to measure the flour?

_____

_____

_____

Build On It!

Write about your favorite sandwich recipe.
Complete **Think About Process: Write a Recipe**
on the Inquiry Flipchart.

Essential Question

How Does Matter Change?

Engage Your Brain!

Find the answer to the question in the lesson.

How did the water turn into ice?

Water becomes ice when heat

_____.

Active Reading

Lesson Vocabulary

1. Preview the lesson.

2. Write the two vocabulary terms here.

_____   _____

Deep Freeze

Taking away or adding heat can change water. Think about making ice. Put water in the freezer. The water freezes into solid ice. Take the ice out of the freezer. It melts into a liquid.

Freezing and melting are reversible changes. When states of matter can change back and forth, it is called a *reversible change*. Some changes to matter, like burning, are not reversible. Burning is an *irreversible change*.

Freezing changes some properties of water. Ice has its own shape. Liquid water does not. Freezing makes water expand. So ice takes up more space than water.

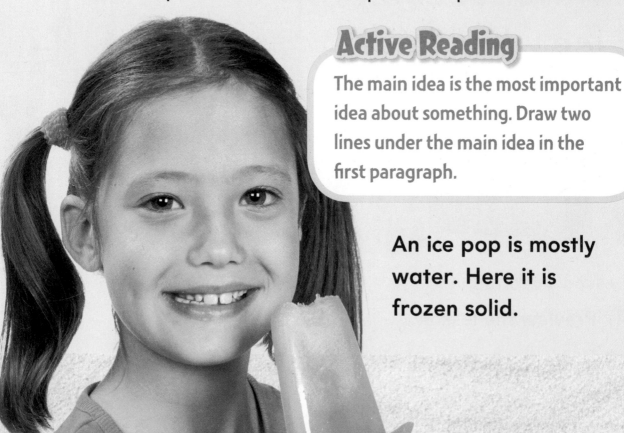

Active Reading

The main idea is the most important idea about something. Draw two lines under the main idea in the first paragraph.

An ice pop is mostly water. Here it is frozen solid.

► Write the name of something that melts.

_____

_____

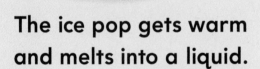

The ice pop gets warm and melts into a liquid.

Do the Math!
Compare Numbers

Circle the answers.

Ice cream has a lot of water in it. It melts faster when the air temperature is higher.

At which temperature will ice cream melt faster?

75 °F or 45 °F

50 °F or 85 °F

Adding and Subtracting

Adding heat can change water. Look at the water in the pot. How does the water change as the stove heats it? The water turns into water vapor. It evaporates into the air. **Evaporation** is the change of water from a liquid to a gas.

Active Reading

Find the sentence that tells the meaning of **evaporation**. Draw a line under the sentence.

evaporation

condensation

How does water vapor change back into water? Just take away heat. Look at the water on the window. The cold window cools water vapor in the air. The water vapor changes to water. It condenses as water drops on the window. **Condensation** is the change of water from a gas to a liquid.

► Circle each math term that helps you understand evaporation and condensation.

Sum It Up!

① Circle It!

Circle the answer.

What happens when you heat liquid water?

evaporation

condensation

_____

What happens when you freeze water?

It shrinks.

It expands.

② Solve It!

Write the answer to the riddle.

You see me as morning dew, or wet drops on a glass. I come around when water changes to a liquid from a gas. What am I?

_____

③ Draw It!

Draw a solid before and after it melts.

Name _____

Word Play

Read the label in each box. Write or draw what happens to water during each change.

Changes to Water

condensation	evaporation
freezing	**melting**

Apply Concepts

In each box, write a phrase that tells the cause of the effect.

Cause | Effect

ice

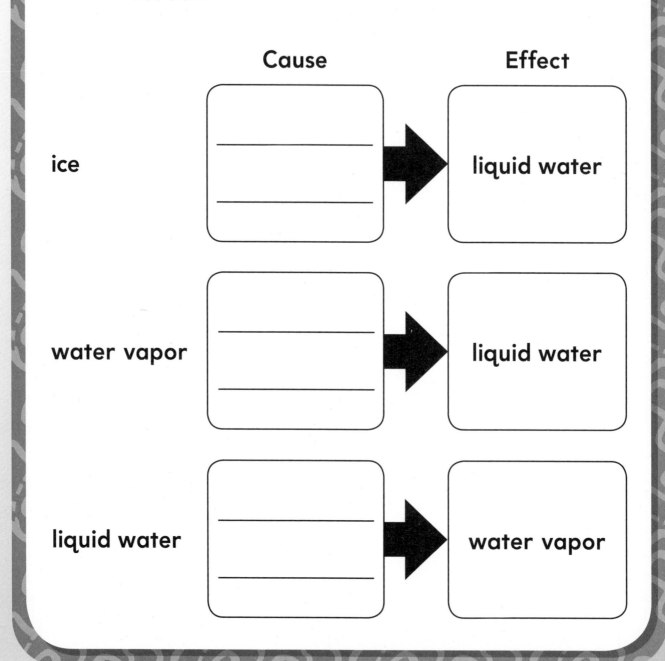

ice → liquid water

water vapor → liquid water

liquid water → water vapor

Take It Home!

Family Members: Have your child point out water changing states at home, such as ice cubes melting or condensation on a glass. Ask him or her to explain how adding or taking away heat causes those changes.

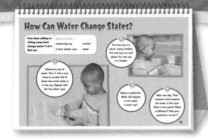

Name _____

Essential Question

How Can Water Change States?

Set a Purpose

Tell what you want to find out in this investigation.

_____

Make Predictions

What do you think will happen to the water?

_____

_____

_____

Think About the Procedure

Why do you measure the water at the beginning of the activity?
Why do you measure again at the end?

_____

_____

Record Your Data

Record the amount of water at the start. At the end, record your observations and measurements.

	Warm Place	Cool Place	Freezer
Start			
End			

Draw Conclusions

Were your predictions correct? How does adding heat and taking away heat affect water? Are these changes to water reversible or irreversible?

_____

_____

_____

Ask More Questions

What other question could you ask about the ways water can change?

_____

1

Dr. Chou was born in Taiwan. She studies physics. Physics is a science that tells about matter and energy.

2

She is a teacher at a university called Georgia Tech.

4

Things to Know About

Dr. Mei-Yin Chou

3

At Georgia Tech, Dr. Chou studies how gases affect solids.

4

She helps girls and women get involved in learning and teaching science.

Word Whiz

▶ **Write the words to match the clues.**

| Taiwan | physics | gases | women | Georgia Tech |

Across

3 Dr. Chou teaches at this university.

Down

1 Dr. Chou helps them learn about science.

2 This science tells about matter and energy.

4 Dr. Chou studies how these affect solids.

5 Dr. Chou was born in this country.

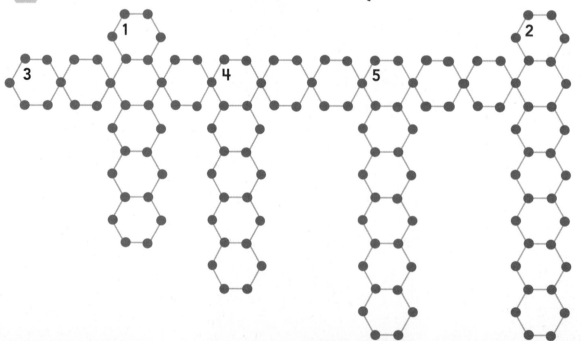

Unit 6 Review

Vocabulary Review

Use the terms in the box to complete the sentences.

condensation
matter
water vapor

1. The change of water from a gas to a liquid is _____.

2. Water in the form of a gas is _____.

3. Anything that has mass and takes up space is _____.

Science Concepts

Fill in the letter of the choice that best answers the question.

4. Taylor sees a balloon filled with air. She knows that the air in the balloon is a gas. How does she know?

   Ⓐ The air is warm.

   Ⓑ The air fills all the space in the balloon.

   Ⓒ The air has its own shape.

5. What happens to water when it freezes?

   Ⓐ It becomes a gas.

   Ⓑ It becomes a liquid.

   Ⓒ It becomes a solid.

6. What is the greatest volume this measuring cup can hold?

Ⓐ $\frac{1}{2}$ cup
Ⓑ 1 cup
Ⓒ 4 cups

7. Which is a solid?
Ⓐ a cloud
Ⓑ a penny
Ⓒ a puddle

8. How is the water changing?

Ⓐ It is melting.
Ⓑ It is evaporating.
Ⓒ It is condensing.

9. Which word tells the amount of space matter takes up?
Ⓐ mass
Ⓑ solid
Ⓒ volume

10. Look at the properties of this object.

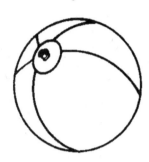

Which of these objects has about the same shape and texture?

Ⓐ
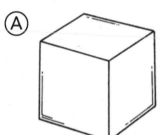

Ⓑ

Ⓒ
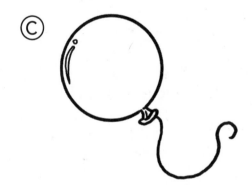

11. How does matter change when it melts?

Ⓐ It turns from a liquid to a gas.

Ⓑ It turns from a solid to a liquid.

Ⓒ It turns from a liquid to a solid.

12. Which is true about all liquids?

Ⓐ All liquids take the shape of their container.

Ⓑ All liquids have their own shape.

Ⓒ All liquids are cold.

13. What can be done with a structure that is made of small wood blocks?

Ⓐ It can be filled with gas.

Ⓑ It can be taken apart and rearranged.

Ⓒ It can take the shape of a container.

Inquiry and the Big Idea
Write the answers to these questions.

14. The same kind of matter is in these three containers.

a. What state of matter is the material? How do you know?

_____

_____

b. How can you measure the volume of the matter in the first container?

_____

c. What would happen to the material if you added heat to it?

_____

d. What would happen to the material if you took heat away from it?

_____

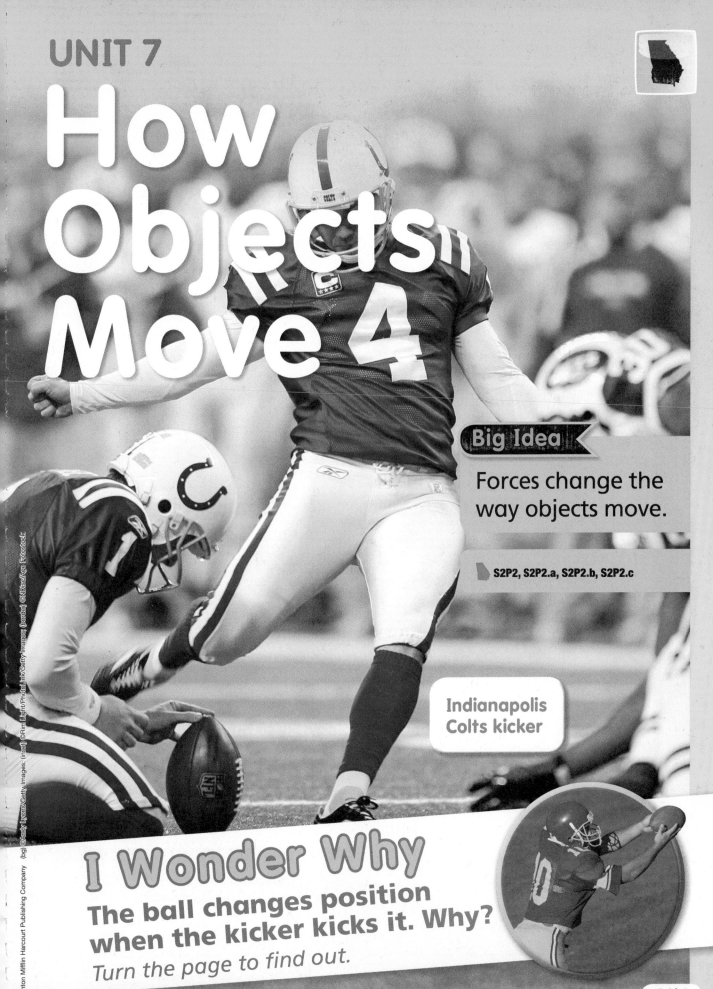

How Objects Move

Big Idea

Forces change the way objects move.

S2P2, S2P2.a, S2P2.b, S2P2.c

Indianapolis Colts kicker

I Wonder Why

The ball changes position when the kicker kicks it. Why?
Turn the page to find out.

Here's Why The ball changes position because of the force from the kicker's foot.

In this unit, you will explore this Big Idea, the Essential Questions, and the Investigations on the Inquiry Flipchart.

Science Notebook

Before you begin each lesson, be sure to write your thoughts about the Essential Question.

© Houghton Mifflin Harcourt Publishing Company (bg) ©Andy Lyons/Getty Images; (inset) ©Tim Light/PhotoLink/Getty Images; (border) ©NDisc/Age Fotostock

Essential Question

How Do Objects Move?

Engage Your Brain!

Find the answer to the question in the lesson.

These Ferris wheel lights look blurry when they are in motion.

How does this Ferris wheel move?

_____

Active Reading

Lesson Vocabulary

1 Preview the lesson.

2 Write the two vocabulary terms here.

_____   _____

Set Things in Motion

The log ride climbs up the hill slowly.

log ride

Look at all of the things in motion! **Motion** is movement. When something is in motion, it is moving.

Planes fly fast. A turtle walks slowly. **Speed** is the measure of how fast something moves.

▶ Circle two things that move fast. Draw an X on two things that move slowly.

244

© Houghton Mifflin Harcourt Publishing Company

Do the Math!
Make a Bar Graph

Pam went on three rides. This graph shows how long she waited for each ride.

Wait Time for Rides

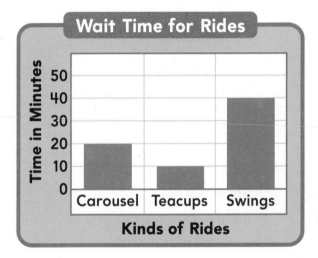

Time in Minutes: 50, 40, 30, 20, 10, 0

Kinds of Rides: Carousel, Teacups, Swings

Use the graph to answer the questions.

1. Which ride had the shortest wait?

_____

2. Tell how you know.

_____

_____

_____

The log ride zooms down the hill fast.

It's Your Move!

Objects can move in many ways.
They can move in a straight line, zigzag,
back and forth, or round and round.

▶ Draw lines below to show the ways
objects can move.

straight line

zigzag

Active Reading

A detail is a fact about a main idea. Draw one line under a detail. Draw an arrow to the main idea it tells about.

back and forth

round and round

① Draw It!

Read the label in each box.
Draw an arrow to show the kind of motion.

back and forth	zigzag	round and round	straight line

② Circle It!

Look at each pair of objects.
Circle the one that goes fast.

Name _____

Word Play

Work your way through the maze to match the word with its meaning.

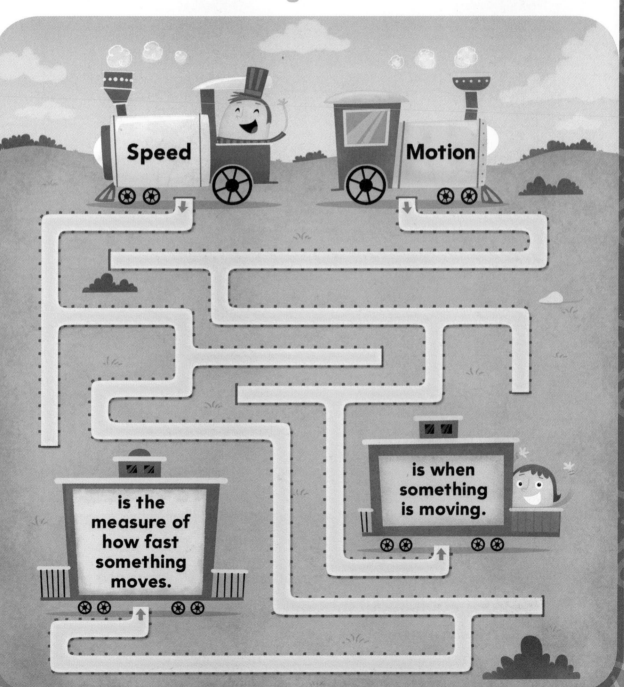

Speed

Motion

is the measure of how fast something moves.

is when something is moving.

Complete the word web below.

The Way Things Move

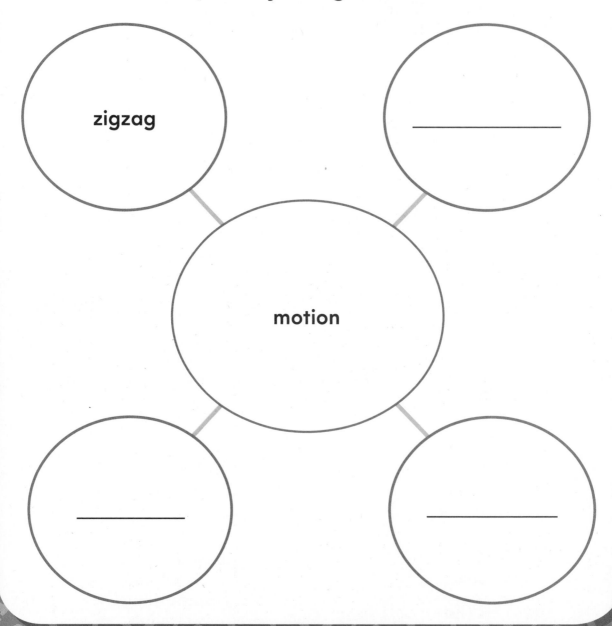

zigzag

_____

motion

_____

_____

Take It Home!

Family Members: See *ScienceSaurus®* for more information about motion.

Name _____

Essential Question

How Can We Change Motion?

Set a Purpose

Tell what you want to figure out in this activity.

_____

_____

Think About the Procedure

1 What do you want to do to the cube?

_____

2 List some ideas for how to push the cube.

_____

_____

3 List some ideas for how to pull the cube.

_____

_____

Record Your Data

Write or draw to show what you did.

Action	What I Did
Push	
Pull	

Draw Conclusions

How do the string, straw, and stick change the motion of the cube?

_____

_____

_____

Ask More Questions

What are some other questions you could ask about changing the motion of a cube?

_____

_____

_____

Fly to the Sky

The First Flight

Wilbur and Orville Wright were brothers and inventors. They flew the first airplane. First, they made designs of their plane. Next, they built it. Then, they tested it. After a few tries, their plane flew. The flight lasted only 12 seconds.

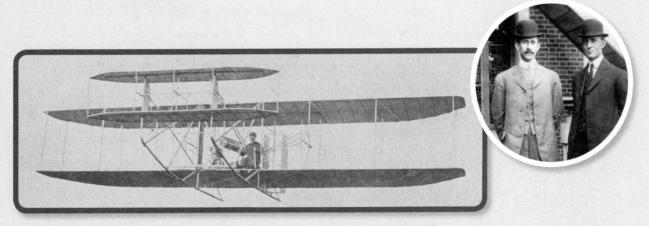

This is one of the Wright Brothers' planes.

Today's planes can fly much longer and have more parts.

Plane Parts

Each part of a plane has a job to do. The wings help lift it. The tail keeps it flying straight. The propeller moves the plane forward.

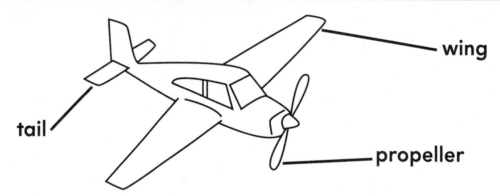

wing

tail

propeller

Use the picture of the plane to answer the questions.

1. Which part keeps the plane flying straight? Circle it.

2. What would happen if the wings on the plane were missing? Explain.

_____

_____

Build On It!

Build your own paper airplanes. Complete **Build It: Paper Airplanes** on the Inquiry Flipchart.

Unit 7 Review

Vocabulary Review

Use the terms in the box to complete the sentences.

| motion |
| push |
| speed |

1. A force that moves an object away from you is a

   _____.

2. The measure of how fast something moves is _____.

3. If something is moving, it is in

   _____.

Science Concepts

Fill in the letter of the choice that best answers the question.

4. Which of these forces is a push?
   - Ⓐ lifting a bag
   - Ⓑ opening a drawer
   - Ⓒ hitting a ball

5. Which is in motion?
   - Ⓐ a bouncing ball
   - Ⓑ a building
   - Ⓒ a sidewalk

6. Which moves the fastest?

Ⓐ

Ⓑ

Ⓒ

7. You need something that can hit a ball over a net. What should you ask?

Ⓐ What material is the ball made of?

Ⓑ What object will put a force on the ball?

Ⓒ What colors are the object and the ball?

8. A player catches a ball in her hand. What puts a force on the ball?

Ⓐ the ball itself

Ⓑ the player's hand

Ⓒ the player's eyes

9. A ball is hanging from a string. You pull the ball back and let it go. What kind of motion does the ball make?

Ⓐ back and forth

Ⓑ round and round

Ⓒ straight line

10. What can a force do?

Ⓐ stop an object

Ⓑ move an object

Ⓒ move or stop an object

11. What force pulls the cars down the hill?

Ⓐ push

Ⓑ gravity

Ⓒ pull

12. Which words describe how a force can change an object's position?

Ⓐ fast or slow

Ⓑ right or left

Ⓒ short or long

Inquiry and the Big Idea

Write the answers to these questions.

13. What do position words describe?

_____

14. Look at the picture.

a. What type of force is being put on the ball? How do you know?

_____

_____

b. Name two things that the force can change about the ball.

_____

Technology and Coding

Have you ever wondered how video games are made? Or how a cell phone works? If so, you might like computer science! Computer science is the study of computer technology.

What Computers Can Do

Computers are machines that take in, manage, and store information. You can solve math problems with a computer. You can make art or music with a computer. Computers can do many things.

Do you recognize these objects? They use computer technology.

Computers are all around you. Even some toasters and cars use computer technology!

_____

_____

_____

_____

Draw another example here.

Let's Talk!

How do computers help solve problems? They follow instructions, or programs, that people make.

Programs are written in a special language, or code. Computers understand the code and follow its instructions. If you learn the code, you can write computer programs, too!

```
dog.speed = 5;
play_sound(woof);
```

People who work in computer science have many skills. They are creative and like to solve problems.

Designing and writing a computer program is like solving a puzzle. The computer follows the program's instructions exactly and in order. If something is missing, the program won't work as planned.

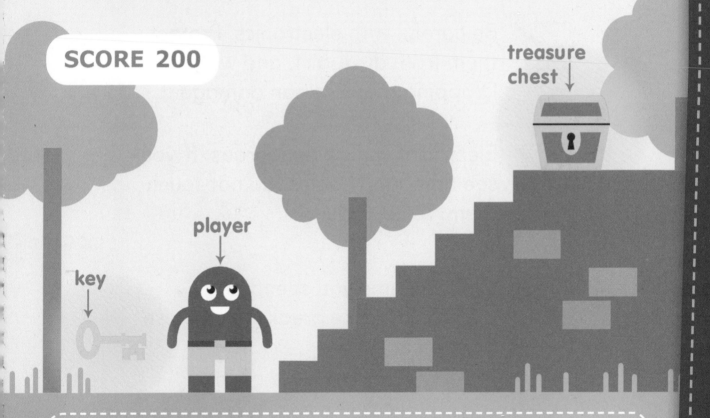

SCORE 200

treasure chest ↓

player ↓

key ↓

How would you move the player to the treasure chest? Explain the steps.

_____

_____

_____

Play it

 Be careful with electronics. Protect them from dust, dirt, and water. Dropping a device can damage it.

 Electricity can be dangerous. If you see damaged cables, do not touch them. Tell an adult.

 Limit the time you spend on electronics. Take breaks to exercise or stretch.

 Talk to your family about rules for the Internet. Do not share private information on your computer or phone. This includes pictures and passwords.

Circle the pictures that show how to use electronics safely. Place an X over the pictures that do not.

Careers in Computing

Do you like art and working with computers? If so, you might enjoy a career in computer animation!

 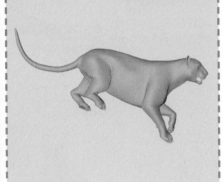 

Animators make characters for movies and video games. They use computer programs to design a character and make its body move.

Interactive Glossary

This Interactive Glossary will help you learn how to spell and pronounce a vocabulary term. The glossary will give you the meaning of the term. It will also show you a picture to help you understand what the term means.

Where you see *Your Turn* write your own words or draw your own picture to help you remember what the term means.

Glossary Pronunciation Key

With every glossary term, there is also a phonetic respelling. A phonetic respelling writes the word the way it sounds. This can help you pronounce new words. Use this key to help you understand the respellings.

Sound	As in	Phonetic Respelling	Sound	As in	Phonetic Respelling
a	bat	(BAT)	oh	over	(OH·ver)
ah	lock	(LAHK)	oo	pool	(POOL)
air	rare	(RAIR)	ow	out	(OWT)
ar	argue	(AR·gyoo)	oy	foil	(FOYL)
aw	law	(LAW)	s	cell	(SEL)
ay	face	(FAYS)		sit	(SIT)
ch	chapel	(CHAP·uhl)	sh	sheep	(SHEEP)
e	test	(TEST)	th	that	(THAT)
	metric	(MEH·trik)		thin	(THIN)
ee	eat	(EET)	u	pull	(PUL)
	feet	(FEET)	uh	medal	(MED·uhl)
	ski	(SKEE)		talent	(TAL·uhnt)
er	paper	(PAY·per)		pencil	(PEN·suhl)
	fern	(FERN)		onion	(UHN·yuhn)
eye	idea	(eye·DEE·uh)		playful	(PLAY·fuhl)
i	bit	(BIT)		dull	(DUHL)
ing	going	(GOH·ing)	y	yes	(YES)
k	card	(KARD)		ripe	(RYP)
	kite	(KYT)	z	bags	(BAGZ)
ngk	bank	(BANGK)	zh	treasure	(TREZH·er)

Interactive Glossary

A

adaptation (ad·uhp·TAY·shuhn)
Something that helps a living thing survive in its environment. (p. 176)

C

communicate
(kuh·MYOO·ni·kayt)
To write, draw, or speak to show what you have learned. (p. 29)

condensation
(kahn·duhn·SAY·shuhn)
The process by which water vapor, a gas, changes into liquid water. (p. 229)

Your Turn

cone (KOHN)
A part of a pine tree and some other plants where seeds form. (p. 146)

D

design process
(dih·ZYN PRAHS·es)

A set of steps that engineers follow to solve problems. (p. 45)

dormancy (DOHR·mehn·see)

A time when plants stop growing. (p. 115)

Your Turn

draw conclusions
(DRAW kuhn·KLOO·zhuhnz)

To use information gathered during an investigation to see whether the results support the hypothesis. (p. 29)

E

engineer (en·juh·NEER)

A person who uses math and science to design technology that solves problems. (p. 44)

Interactive Glossary

environment
(en·ᴠʏ·ruhn·muhnt)
All the living and nonliving things in a place. (pp. 64, 164)

evaporation
(ee·vap·uh·ʀᴀʏ·shuhn)
The process by which liquid water changes into water vapor, a gas. (p. 228)

Your Turn

F

food chain
(FOOD CHAYN)
A path that shows how energy moves from plants to animals.
(p. 170)

force (FOHRS)
An action that changes the motion or position of an object. (p. 252)

germinate (JER·muh·nayt)
To start to grow. (p. 142)

Your Turn

G

gas (GAS)
A state of matter that fills all the space of its container. (p. 215)

H

hypothesis (hy·PAHTH·uh·sis)
A statement that you can test. (p. 27)

Interactive Glossary

I

inquiry skills
(IN·**kwer**·ee SKILZ)
The skills people use to find out information. (p. 4)

investigate (in·VES·**tuh**·gayt)
To plan and do a test to answer a question or solve a problem. (p. 26)

L

larva (LAHR·**vuh**)
Another name for a caterpillar. (p. 135)

Your Turn

life cycle (LYF SY·**kuhl**)
Changes that happen to an animal or a plant during its life. (p. 129)

1

2

3

liquid (LIK·wid)
A state of matter that takes the shape of its container. (p. 214)

mass (MAS)
The amount of matter in an object. (p. 210)

matter (MAT·er)
Anything that takes up space and has mass. (p. 210)

Your Turn

M

magnify (MAG·neh·fye)
To make something look bigger. (p. 88)

Interactive Glossary

metamorphosis
(met·uh·MAWR·fuh·sis)
A series of changes in appearance that some animals go through. (p. 131)

migrate (MY·grayt)
To travel from one place to another and back again. (p. 115)

moon (MOON)
A large sphere, or ball of rock revolving around a planet. (p. 84)

motion (MOH·shun)
Movement. (p. 244)

Your Turn

phases (FAY·zuz)

How much of the moon we see as it circles the Earth. (p. 103)

pollen (POL·uhn)

A powder that flowers need to make seeds. Some small animals help carry pollen from one flower to another. (p. 169)

Your Turn

property (PRAH·per·tee)

One part of what something is like. Color, shape, size, and texture are each a property. (p. 210)

pull (PUHL)

Moves an object closer to you. (p. 252)

pupa (PYOO·puh)

The part of a life cycle when a caterpillar changes into a butterfly. (p. 135)

Interactive Glossary

push (PUSH)
Moves an object away from you. (p. 252)

R

reproduce (ree·pruh·DOOS)
To have young, or more living things of the same kind. (p. 128)

Your Turn

resource (REE·sawrs)
Anything people can use to meet their needs. (p. 196)

S

science tools
(SY·uhns TOOLZ)
The tools people use to find out information. (p. 14)

season (SEE·**zuhn**)

A time of year that has a certain kind of weather. The four seasons are spring, summer, fall, and winter. (p. 112)

Your Turn

seedling (SEED·**ling**)

A young plant. (p. 143)

seed (SEED)

The part of a plant that new plants may grow from. (p. 140)

shadow (SHA·**doh**)

A dark place made where an object blocks light. (p. 99)

Interactive Glossary

solid (SAHL·id)
The only state of matter that has its own shape. (p. 213)

Your Turn

star (STAR)
A large ball of hot gases that gives off light and heat. (p. 80)

sun (SUHN)
The star closest to Earth. (p. 80)

speed (SPEED)
The measure of how fast something moves. (p. 244)

T

tadpole (TAD·pohl)

A young frog that comes out of an egg and has gills to take in oxygen from the water. (p. 130)

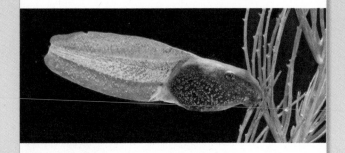

Your Turn

technology (tek·NOL·uh·jee)

What engineers make to meet needs and solve problems. (p. 58)

telescope (TEH·leh·skohp)

A tool that helps us magnify things in the sky. (p. 88)

thermometer (ther·MAHM·uht·ter)

A tool used to measure temperature. (p. 15)

Interactive Glossary

V

volume (VAHL·**yoom**)
The amount of space that matter takes up. (p. 214)

Your Turn

W

water vapor
(WAW·ter VAY·per)
Water in the form of a gas. (p. 216)

Index

Index

Index

M

Index

Index

solving problems, 35–36. *See also* **design process**

sound, as energy, 241

space, need for, 165

speed, 244, R12
  change in, 254–255, 258–259
  motion and, 244–245

sphere, 85

spring, 113–114

sprinkler irrigation, 155–156

star(s), 80, 82–83, 86–87, 104, R12
  brightness, 82, 86–87
  observing, 88
  size, 82, 86–87
  sun, 82

states of matter, 233–234
  gases, 207–209, 212, 215–217, 228–229
  liquids, 15, 207, 212, 214, 216–217, 227–229
  solids, 207, 212–213, 216–217, 226

State Your Hypothesis, 221

stem, 142

S.T.E.M. (Science, Technology, Engineering, and Mathematics), 119, 155, 189, 223, 267

See also **Engineering and Technology**
  Bringing Water to Plants, 155
  Fly to the Sky: The First flight, 267
  Fly to the Sky: Plane Parts, 268
  Kitchen Technology, 223–224
  See the Light: Bright Ideas, 120
  See the Light: Compare Flashlights, 119
  Technology and the Environment: Dams, 189–190

storms, 113

straight line motion, 246

summer, 113–114
  stars in, 104
  storms in, 113

sun, 77, R12
  apparent movement of, 98, 109–110
  in daytime sky, 80–81
  Earth's movement around, 94
  shadows and, 98–99, 109–110
  as star, 80, 82
  sunspots, 93

sundial, 100–101

sunlight
  in food chain, 170

  hours of daylight, 112–113
  need for, 165
  seasonal changes in, 114–115
  shadows and, 99
  sundial, 100–101

sunspots, 93

survival
  adaptations for, 180–183
  animals, 182–183
  plants, 176–177, 180–181, 187–188

table, interpreting, 141

tadpole, 130–131, R13

tape measure, 17

technology, 57–65, R13. *See also* **Engineering and Technology**
  airplanes, 267–268
  bathroom, 58–59
  batteries, 64–65
  coding, 273–277
  computers, 273–277
  cooking tools, 223–224
  dams, 189–190
  design process, 41, 43–51
  environment and, 189–190
  home, 60–61
  improving, 69–70

Index

irrigation, 155
kitchen, 223–224
safety and, 62–63
telescope, 88–89, 93–94, R13
temperature, 15
Celsius scale, 21–22
melting and, 227
seasonal changes in, 112–115
testing
in design process, 50
in science, 27–28, 30–31
texture, 210–211
thermometer, 13, 15, R13
Think About the Procedure, 23, 35, 55, 69, 95, 109, 153, 187, 221, 233, 265
third quarter moon, 103
Three Laws of Motion, 263–264
timer, 223
tools, 14
cooking, 223–224
measuring, 15–17
science, 13–17, 23–24, R10
telescope, 88–89, 93–94

trash, 196
trees
apple, 144–145
dormancy, 115
in fall, 114
forest fires and, 193
life span for, 145
pine, 146–147
replanting, 197
seedlings, 147
in spring, 114
in summer, 114
in winter, 114
21st Century Skills: Technology and Coding, 273–277

up, 256

volume, 214, R13

water
for animals, 115, 164
condensation, 229
dams, 189–190, 194–195
evaporation, 228
in food chain, 170

freezing, 226
heat and, 225–229
ice, 225
irrigation, 155–156
melting, 227
for plants, 155–156, 164
salt, 214
states of, 216–217, 225–229, 233–234
water vapor, 216–217, 228–229, R13
weathering, 192
weather patterns, seasonal changes in, 111–115
weight, measuring, 16
Why It Matters, 30–31, 64–65, 88–89, 258–259
width, 17
winter, 104, 111–112, 114–115
Word Meaning, 4, 6, 8, 44, 58, 164, 196, 209, 215, 228, 253
Wright, Orville, 267
Wright, Wilbur, 267

Zavala, Maria Elena, 151
zigzag (motion), 246